MIRACLES
STILL HAPPEN

Are you ready for a Miracle? This book will help you to discover your rights and also what was promised to you by God himself.

Believe God for your Miracle today.
For with God All Things Are Possible.

I am believing God that by the end of reading this book you will have a great testimony to share with others of what God has done for you.

ROBIN DINNANAUTH

xulon
PRESS

Copyright © 2008 by Robin Dinnanauth
First Printing © 2007

MIRACLES STILL HAPPEN
by Robin Dinnanauth

Printed in the United States of America

ISBN 978-160477-412-2

All rights reserved solely by the author. The author guarantees all contents are original and do not infringe upon the legal rights of any other person or work. No part of this book may be reproduced in any form without the permission of the author. The views expressed in this book are not necessarily those of the publisher.

Unless otherwise indicated, Bible quotations are taken from the New International Version (NIV). Copyright © 1973, 1978, 1984 by International Bible Society.

www.xulonpress.com

MIRACLES
STILL HAPPEN

Jesus Christ the same yesterday, today and forever.

What he has done two thousand years ago, he is still doing the same today.

CONTENTS

	Acknowledgment	ix
	About the Author	xi
	Introduction	xiii
1	Miracles in the times of desperation	17
2.	God promised Miracles	29
3	Hindrances that can Block your Miracle	39
4	How to receive your Miracle	49
5	God Has the Power to Heal and change things	57
6	Miracles through faith	65
7	Miracles through the Word	71
8	Miracles of Financial Blessings	79

9	Miracles of Deliverance	91
10	Miracles of the Old Testament	99
11.	Miracles of the New Testament	105
12.	Declaration	117
13.	Plan of Salvation	119
14.	Prayer for Salvation	123

ACKNOWLEDGMENTS

With a grateful heart I would like to say special thanks to some very important people in my life who have help me tremendously.

To My beautiful wife Veronica, who stood by my side and supported me in the past eleven years. Veronica has been my prayer warrior, my best friend and most important my faithful partner who is always there to encourage me to go on and finish whatever I am doing. Veronica is a great woman of God and I love her with my every being. To you my loving wife: it's a miracle how we first met and it will continued to be a miracle as God continued to keep us together as we will continue to work to build his kingdom. I love you and thank you for standing by my side and for your total dedication and help while I was writing this book.

To my handsome looking boys Justin and Josiah, who have given me time to write this book and understand me when I needed some quiet time alone. I would like to specially dedicate this book to them. Justin and Josiah other than My Father and God both of you are my joy and blessings. Your mom and I love you both I bless you for understanding us when we have to leave you with grandma sometimes to do ministry. Great will be your reward. I pray a blessing on you my sons. Keep serving the Lord and do exploits for him he will work miracles for the two of you.

To my director Al Williams and his wife Rani Williams, of Robin Healing Ministries WOW! You both have been an inspiration to me. Thank you for your encouraging words and for pushing me to get this book done. Rev. Al I would like to thank you for all that you have done to help me and my ministry and also for your hard work in all my projects.

To all the staff of Robin Healing Ministries and Emmanuel Full Gospel Assemblies: Thank you for your hard work. I would like to say special thanks to all of you for understanding me especially in my difficult times. Special thanks to Rev. Roger Hans for holding the fort for me when I am busy and not forgetting the night prayer and intercessory group who keep praying for me.

To Xulon press and the entire production team, thank you very much for believing in me and to publish my first daily encouragement and prayer journal Every Day with Jesus. Thank you for your hard work in publishing this book. Blessings!

And more important I would like to thank the Lord my God and savior Jesus Christ who has been my shield and banner and my miracle worker. Glory be to his name. Amen.

About the Author

Robin Dinnanauth is an active Evangelist ministering the Gospel of the Lord Jesus Christ and demonstrating God's Healing and Deliverance power in the USA and South America. He has been used mightily by God in Healing and Deliverance, preaching in Crusades and Revival meetings. He is out in the front, battling Satan, leading the charge against demonic forces that appear to have so many souls in torment. He is also the Author of best-selling Prayer Journal "Every Day with Jesus."

As a highly sought-after crusader and revival speaker who God has raised up as a prophetic voice to the world, Robin is calling people to Jesus Christ through the good news of the Gospel and the power of the blood of the Lamb. Thousands experience the saving, healing and delivering message of Jesus Christ as he ministers hope to the sick, the afflicted and the hurting.

He is known for his dynamic and anointed prayer, healing and deliverance ministry. An Ordained Minister, Pastor, Overseer, and Sought-after conference speaker. He is the founder of Emmanuel Full Gospel Assemblies of Churches, Robin Healing Ministries and Emmanuel Bible Training Institute.

INTRODUCTION

WHEN I look around and see so many people that are suffering from sickness, diseases, oppression and depression, Having problems financially, physically and emotionally I wonder if they know that MIRACLE STILL HAPPENS.

There are so many people that are broken and gave up hope when life goes off course with them. When a person's spirit is broken, there is no more fire of passion or desire left within them for God and even for their own lives. This often leaves a person without the motivation to do the will of God, to reach toward the things that are before them, or sometimes even to live at all.

When one's spirit is broken within them because of the situation in lives, there is no JOY, there is no HOPE, if there is laughter at all it is superficial, and more often there is no FAITH.

Many things can cause such a situation in our life or cause our spirits to be broken within us:

- An accumulation of trouble and stress in our lives.
- Prayers that seemingly go unanswered.

- Questions that remains unanswered for long periods of time.
- Problems that remains unresolved.
- Broken marriages
- Financial difficulties

These are but a few of the multitude of things that can break our spirits and sap the passion of life and God from us. But even in the midst of broken spirits – Miracle still happens. By the time you finish reading this book you will be able to believe God for your miracle. Because Miracles are promised to those who know him and personally serve him, the bible says "God will not withhold any good from them that love him."

The book of Ezekiel 11:19 says "I will put a new spirit in you." God didn't say that He was going to remodel, revamp, redo and fix up the Old spirit. He said in his word your life would be so great that He would put a new spirit in you. It is an error on our part to limit our expectation to just an emotional refurbishing. God is ready to do a new thing in your life and spirit. He is a miracle working God, He's Alpha and Omega the beginning and the end.

According to my research never in history has the health of mankind been affected as it is today. Major diseases are killing our children while incurable illnesses are wrecking havoc on the lives of the young and old alike. Countless billions of dollars are spent each year in the United States in health care cost and still there are diseases for which there is no known cure.

It is not enough that we are contending with illnesses and sickness of a physical nature. Now we are contending with illnesses of an emotional and mental nature as well. A New York scientist studying mental illness reported to the United Nations committee that up to thirty percent of the world's population is suffering from some form of emotional or mental disorder.

It is a challenge to lose your own health or watch a loved one whose health begins to deteriorate. Irritation sets in and hopelessness begins to prevail. Some folks begin to feel like they have lost their usefulness to their families and to God because of their broken health. But the good news is that even if your health fails, God will not fail. MIRACLE STILL HAPPENS. For the bible says he is God in the times of trouble.

The book of Isaiah 53:5 says ***"He was wounded for our transgressions, He was bruised for our iniquities, the chastisement of our peace was upon him: and with His stripes we are healed."***

Hundreds of scriptural references recorded in both Old and New Testaments tell us that God is still a Healer and Miracle Worker. From the curing of blood diseases to the raising of the dead, nothing was, or is, impossible with God. The bible says he (GOD) is the same yesterday, today and forever more.

James 5:14-15 says "Is any sick among you? Let him call for the elders of the church: and let them pray over him, anointing him with oil in the name of the Lord and the prayer of faith shall save the sick." That is a promise for healing.

Even when your health is broken God is your healer. The scars on His back are proof of your healing. Look beyond the pain, look beyond the symptoms, look even beyond the doctor's prognosis – and see your healer sending healing to your life. For when your health is broken God is with you still and is and will always be "your God."

Regardless of where you are in life or what your particular "Broken Place" might be. God will be God right there in times of need he is a miracle working God. There is no problem too great for Him. There is no broken place that God can't fix. He is the same God that healed the woman with the issue of blood and he is that same God that is doing miracles today. Cast your cares on Him for He cares for you. There is a song that I love so much that has these words "He's the God of the mountains, He's God of the valley, when things go wrong he'll make them right, Because he's the God of the good times and still God in the bad times, the God of the day and he's God in the night." God never change. We are the ones that change. But he never did.

I am believing God by the time you finish reading this book, that you have received your miracle. Trust and you will see that God is a miracle working God, because MIRACLE STILL HAPPENS.

CHAPTER ONE

MIRACLES IN THE TIMES OF DESPERATION

All Things are Possible with God.

*But he was wounded for our transgressions,
he was bruised for our iniquities;
the chastisement of our peace was upon him;
and with his stripes we are healed.*
Isaiah 53:5

WHAT IS MIRACLE - Miracle is a historical event or natural phenomena that appears to violate natural laws but that reveal God to the eye of faith at the same time. A valuable way of understanding the meaning of miracles is to examine the various terms for miracles used in the Bible. A miracle also has been defined as a work wrought by a divine power for a divine purpose by means beyond the reach of man.

Miracles still happen today!

There has never been so much hurt, sickness or disease evident among people as there is today. Relationships are crumbling all around us; people are dying from cancer, aids, diabetes, high blood pressure etc. Painful and hurtful words are being hurled like daggers at one another. Loneliness strikes the hearts of men and women with unprecedented devastation.

We reach a place in life that we can't find happiness on our jobs, in our homes and even at our churches because we're too busy trying to resolve the issues of brokenness, sickness, diseases, oppression and depression.

When you reach the place of brokenness you can take comfort that God is still doing miracles. God never thinks of us as being dysfunctional because of our sickness or diseases. When our hearts are broken within us – God never sees us as unattractive or undesirable. He said in his word *"The Lord draws nigh unto them that are of a broken heart!" Psalm 34:19*

In the book of Luke 4:18 we find Jesus echoing the word spoken in prophecy by Isaiah the prophet ***"The Spirit of the Lord God is upon me, because He hath anointed me to preach the gospel to the poor: and He hath sent me to heal the brokenhearted."***

It doesn't matter the cause of your sickness. When your problems and situations are getting worse, God will draw close to you. Even when you don't feel you can draw close to Him – He is drawing close to you and when God draws nigh unto you – He will heal your sickness and work a miracle in your situations and solve your problems.

One of the most beautiful scriptures in the Bible is found in John 3:16. In this passage of scripture we are made to understand that God viewed the sorrowful condition of the world, observed the despair among its inhabitants, and beheld their sinfulness yet He loved man enough to send, not just any redeemer, but He sent His only begotten Son. Who was wounded for our transgression, bruised for our iniquities, took stripes on his back for our healing and carried our miracles.

This was done that, by God's help man might rise above his despair, whether it was caused by sin, failures, or just the cares of life, you need to live according to the promises of God, just live a life of glorious liberty.

Jesus, himself, said that He has come to seek and to save the lost. He did not come to celebrate the good works of mankind, nor did He come to mingle with all the law abiding righteous folks. He came to bring help to those that are hurting and give miracle of deliverance and healing to troubled lives.

It would be nice if things always went well in our lives and our lives consisted only of celebrating great blessings. But more times than not we find our lives in NEED of help and guidance from God. Our lives get tangled in the affairs of this life, we miss the will of God, and we fail to recognize all that God has done for us, or we even sin and come short of God's glory – the list can go on and on.

Regardless of how desperate we are or where we are in life or what circumstances surround us, there is good news from the throne of God. He promises us miracles.

Some of which God has promised us are:
- The Miracle of Salvation
- The Miracle of Peace, Joy and Happiness
- The Miracle of Blessings – Financially, Physically and emotionally.
- The Miracle of Healing and deliverance

There was a moment of desperation in my personal life when I experience the Miracle of Healing and deliverance. This is my testimony of a Miracle.

In times of desperation he's still a miracle working God.

I was one year old suffering with Anemia, my mother was so afraid of me being dead with no hope from the doctor, and don't know what next to do she decided to turn to an old Christian woman who has been sharing tracts and talking about Jesus Christ in our community and every where she went.

Being born in a Hindu home and my family being Hindu it was a tough decision for my mother to make to call upon a Christian for help but with no hope from the doctor and don't know what next to do she decided to call upon this old Christian lady who always talks about how Jesus is a miracle worker, who can heal, save and deliver people from their distress.

Without hesitation the old Christian woman came to our house and laid her hand upon me and prayed "Lord Jesus, Please heal this Child and use him to bring salvation to this household, let his parents see that you are a miracle worker, Amen." As she finished praying, she encouraged my mother to take me to church and serve the Lord.

At age four my mother started to send me to Sunday school at a Pentecostal Church. Church was not an interest for her or my family because Hinduism was what they believed in. At age seven, I was attacked by a skin disease on both of my feet. Again my mother would take me to every dermatologist that she knew or heard about. Things grew worse and worse for me.

With frustration and don't know what to do my mother took me to live with my grandmother, who was a Lutheran, she loved the Lord and has been serving God faithfully in the Lutheran church. Living with my grandmother, she recognized that the hands of the Lord was upon my life and started to believe God for my healing. One day she heard of a missionary that came to a little Pentecostal church in her community and he was having a few nights of Healing service. She decided to take me to the healing service. By then I was nine years old and clearly remembered that the preacher was saying "I am here because the Holy Ghost sent me here to heal the sick and Deliver those that are possessed with demons."

I was afraid of what I was seeing. People were falling down under the power of the Holy Spirit, people were screaming and I thought for a minute I wanted to leave but with the faith of my grandmother she told me to wait he will call and pray with me. So my grandmother started to believe God for my miracle. As soon as the preacher called me my grandmother took me up and requested a prayer for my healing. The missionary preacher then laid his hands on me and I could remember he said "God want to heal you so that he can use you."

At that time he asked me if I would like to confess Jesus as my Lord and Savior. Without any hesitation I answered yes immediately, because I was very desperate for my healing. He asked me to repeat the sinner's prayer and prayed for my healing. That day I received the Lord as my personal Lord and Savior. One week later the disease from both of my feet disappeared and I was totally healed and I am healed up to this day. It was a miracle. God did a miracle for me and I know he still does miracles today.

I was desperate for my healing and in the midst of my desperation God just showed up and healed me. It took me years to realize that the hand of God was upon my life and the devil knew that, so he was trying to destroy me with sickness and diseases. When the Anointing and Call of God is upon your life the devil will try to stop you and derail you from the destiny God has put you on. You have to remember that the devil cannot destroy or kill you, he can't touch you. When Job was being attacked by the devil, God warned him that he can touch anything that Job has BUT he cannot touch his life. God has given us life and life more abundantly; he has invested in us an anointing for his honor and glory. So the devil will continue to try to destroy the anointing God has given you. You think that king Pharaoh was afraid of the two year old boys in the New Testament. No, he was afraid of the deliverer he heard about (He was afraid that a King was born). The devil doesn't want to destroy you he wants to destroy the anointing that is on you.

The devil could not destroy me with sickness or disease because God has a plan for my life. When God has a plan for your life the devil will try to mess with you but little did he realize that "Greater is he that is in me than he that is in the world. For the bible says "No weapon that fashioned against me will prosper."

When you least expect God will show up. He is a God that never lies. His word will never return void to him. The bible says that heaven and earth will pass away but not one jot of his word will pass away. There are hundreds of scripture in the bible that promise us that God will works wonders and miracle for his people. You have to remember that you have been created in his own likeness and image. His main purpose for creating us is that he can commune with us. God inhabits the praises of his people. He purpose in his heart that none should perished but all shall come to repentance and have everlasting life. He created us perfectly. God is concerned with your well being. He wants his children to be whole. There will be times when desperation kicks in and the devil try to tell you that God forgot you. That is the moment when you need to remember the word of God and his promises.

Don't you ever give up on God. He has a plan for your life. He will turn your mourning into dancing again. There are times when you will feel that God has forgotten you and he lift up his hands and surrender on you, but that doesn't mean that he gave up on you. He wanted to lift his hands up and show you the nail scars just to remind you of what he has done for you. He want to show you his nail scared hands for you to remember what the prophet Isaiah prophesied in the book of Isaiah 53:5.

Even when I was a child I realized that God can heal. I believe him for my healing and he did it for me. Today God has been using me in the Healing and Deliverance Ministry. God has done a miracle for me. I am preaching the Gospel of the Lord Jesus Christ to the lost, demonstrating his healing power to the sick and delivering those that are possessed by demonic spirits through the power of his Name and set those that are in captivity free in Jesus Name. I can testify that God still do miracles.

For my healing, every prayer was answered, from that old Christian woman to the missionary preacher who God has used to prophesy over my life and prayed for my second healing. God is willing to heal from anemia to skin disease. His words declare -

Ezekiel 16:6 *And when I passed by thee, and saw thee polluted in thine own blood, I said unto thee, when thou wast in thy blood, Live; yea I said unto thee when thus wast in thy blood, Live.*

Joel 3:21 *For I will cleanse their blood that I have not cleansed; for the LORD dwelleth in Zion.*

To receive a miracle it takes faith and believing in the power of Jesus Christ. For you to receive your miracle, the first thing you must do is to activate the power of believing so that you can receive your miracle and believe God for what he has promised. I know that God has promised us healing, deliverance, blessings and breakthrough. If you believe you will receive. Will you be able to believe God for your loved ones healing, deliverance and salvation? God hears and answer every prayer. When sickness comes in your life or loved ones lives I want you to know don't you ever give up! Because God still do miracles. The bible says "he is the same yesterday, today and for evermore."

One thing you need to know is that God wants you to be whole! The devil want to make us believe that God has caused sickness upon us, and that is a way of putting judgment on us. That is a lie from hell itself. God does not cause illness. In the book of Acts 10:38 states, *God anointed Jesus of Nazareth with the Holy Ghost and with power: who went about doing good, and healing all that were oppressed of the devil; for God was with him.* Sickness is an oppression of the devil, and Jesus came against sickness and disease with healing in the touch of His hands and in every word He spoke. He spent two-thirds of His ministry healing people and making them whole.

You were not born to be sick or diseased. Healing can be yours through Christ who said, *"The Spirit of the Lord is upon me, because he hath anointed me to preach the gospel to the poor; he hath sent me to heal the brokenhearted, to preach deliverance to the captives, and recov-*

ering of sight to the blind." **Luke 4:18. Matthew 8:17 says, "Jesus *Himself took our infirmities, and bore our sicknesses."*** Because of Jesus' death on the cross we have a Bible right to healing and health. God wants you to be a whole person. Reach out and receive your healing today, in Jesus name. Miracles still happen and he still does miracles.

In October, 2004 doctors diagnose my mother with thyroid, hypotension and diabetes. She was schedule for a surgery because she was loosing her voice, her blood pressure went up and her blood sugar was rocket high. My father was told by the doctor to sign a document that if anything should go wrong they are not responsible. I refused to let my father sign because I know that God still does miracles.

In the moment of despair God remind me of the miracle of the Woman with an Issue of Blood.

Matthew 9:20-22 ***And behold, a woman, which was diseased with an issue of blood twelve years, came behind him, and touched the hem of his garment; for she said within herself, If I may but touch his garment, I shall be whole. But Jesus turned about, and when he saw her, he said Daughter, be of good comfort; thy faith hath made thee whole. And the woman was made whole from that hour.***

I refused to accept a surgery for my mother, I told my father not to sign that document and I went before the Lord, because I know he is touched by our infirmities and know that he still does miracles. On October 10, 2004 my mother accepted the Lord Jesus Christ as her personal Lord and Savior and I anointed her with oil laid my hands on her and rebuked that thyroid, hypotension and diabetes in Jesus Name. My mother received her healing and she is now serving the Lord faithfully and is a staff of the Robin Healing Ministries telling others that God Can and Still Do Miracles. Glory be to God.

What the devil meant for bad, God meant well, my mother's sickness has brought my entire family to Jesus Christ. Today my entire family is serving the Lord for his Goodness and mercy. When a situation arises in your life; God will receive glory out of it, because he will prove himself as the miracle worker. HOW? Bear in mind if you never get sick, how can you experience the miracle of healing, if you never suffer with financial problems how can you prove that God is Jehovah Jireh your provider.

I remember while praying in my living room one night the telephone rang and I was being called to go the hospital to repeat the Lord prayer with a woman who was on a life support machine and to pull the plug. As I left my house and was on my way to the hospital I said "God you're using me in healing and deliverance why should I do this." And the Holy Spirit spoke to my heart and said "Do you believe in Miracle?" and I quickly responded "yes I do" and immediately I realize that I need to go pray for this woman's healing and not to go and pull the plug out of the life support machine. As I got there I anointed her with oil, laid my hands on her and prayed a prayer of faith for her healing. The family watched as I prayed, and was preparing for me to pull the plug. Little did they realize that God was healing their sister and she started to breathe. Today she is alive and well serving the Lord. God did a miracle for her and he still does miracles today. He is willing to perform your miracle today if you will trust and believe him because that is what he promised, that he will heal, deliver and set free.

Jesus is touched by the very feeling of our infirmities. When we cry he cries, when we're hungry he's hungry. When we're hurting he's hurting.

What's keeping you from your miracle? Luke 1:37 says ***"For with God nothing shall be impossible."*** If God is able to do all things and all things are possible with him then what are you waiting on. We're serving an awesome and mighty God. He is as close as the mention of his name he is not a little helpless baby in the manger. There is no lack to our God and his mighty power. He is not some gray-headed grandfather who walks with some weather beaten staff in his hands. He is a God that works wonders and perform miracles, and is just a prayer away; when you think that the moon is just one hundred miles away from earth and Pluto is the most distance planet in our solar system its nearly ten billion miles away. Your miracle is just a prayer away.

The bible says that he will not withhold anything good from them that love him. God promised you, that he will heal in his word.

CHAPTER TWO

GOD PROMISED HEALING

"Who Himself bore our sins in His own body on the tree, that we, having died to sins might live for righteousness-by whose stripes you were healed."
1 Peter 2:24

Promise – promise is a solemn pledge to perform or grant a specified thing. God did not have to promise anything to sinful people. But the fact that almost all biblical promises are those made by God to human beings indicates that His nature is characterized chiefly by grace and faithfulness.

God promise every one of his children's healing. In his word he said Healing is the children bread. He invested the power in us to choose for ourselves whether or not we want our healing. You don't have to beg for it, it's yours as a child of God. It was promised to you. All you have to do is to ask for it.

The bible says in the book of James call upon the Elders let them lay hands and pray for you. James 5:13-15 ***Is anyone among you suffering? Let him pray. Is anyone*** *cheerful? Let him sing psalms. Is anyone among you sick? Let him call for the elders of the church, and let them pray over him, Anointing him with oil in the name of the Lord. And the prayer of faith will save the sick, and the Lord will raise him up. And if he has committed sins, he will be forgiven.*

Healing is there for you, it was given to us at the cross, all you need to do is to reach out and receive it in Jesus' Name. God is a man that never lies. He keeps his promise from generation to generation.

The Lord spoke to Joshua and promises him possession in Joshua 1:3 *"Every place that the sole of your foot shall tread upon I have given you, as I said to Moses."*

God kept his promise to Joshua and gave him that which was promised to him. Joshua 21:43-45 *So the Lord God gave to Israel all the land of which He had sworn to give to their fathers, and they took possession of it and dwelt in it. The Lord gave them rest all around, according to all that He had sworn to their fathers. And not a man of all their enemies stood against them; the Lord delivered all their enemies into their hand. Not a word failed of any good thing which the Lord had spoken to the house of Israel. All came to pass.*

Your healing and your Miracle has been promised to you. Joshua was very faithful to the Lord and he obeyed his commands. Are you faithful to the Lord? There are many times people ask me, "I have been seeking the Lord for my healing but I am still waiting. Can you tell me if God still does miracles?" Oh of course yes, he still does miracles. I am a living testimony to that. He did it for me personally. I have experienced his miracles and healing power in my own life. It's a miracle for me to live.

He promises you that he will heal you, are you ready to receive what he promised? Or did you ever ask him to heal you as he promise? There are times in our lives when we want a miracle but never ask God for it. This reminds me of a fifty two year old man who was praying for a miracle but never acted with faith.

There was once a man who fell sick and was in the hospital. So a preacher of the gospel went to visit him and ask him if he believes that God hears and answer prayers. He replied and said "well I don't know if God does answer prayer because I have been praying for twenty two years now to win the lotto but God never hears my prayer so I don't think he will hear yours today." And the preacher of the gospel replied "how many times have you purchased a lotto ticket?" His reply was "I NEVER PURCHASED ONE."

That is the problem with many Christians today they know the promises of God, but never activate the power of asking in their lives. The bible says Ask and it shall be given, seek and you shall find, knock and it shall be opened unto you.

The scripture says in the book of Isaiah *"For the Lord God will help me; therefore shall I not be confounded; therefore have I seen my face like a flint and I know that I shall not be ashamed."* Isaiah 50:7. God is waiting on us to act by faith. So that he can give what he has promised you. We are sitting and waiting for a miracle but never ask for it. Well you may ask how I can ask for my Miracle. The answer is simple the bibles say in Proverbs 4:20-22 *"My son, attend to my words; incline thine ear unto my sayings. Let them not depart form thine eyes; keep them in the midst of thine heart. For they are life unto those that find them, and health to all their flesh."*

There are times when the devil will try to tell you that you are not qualified for the promises of God. God will not give you a miracle because you are not serving him long enough. The devil is a liar. God is no respecter of Persons. If you believe you shall receive.

The bible says that a Gentile woman shows her faith to Jesus. In Matthew 15:21-28 a gentile woman's daughter was possessed with a spirit and she came to Jesus and said "Master my daughter is severely demon-possessed." And Jesus disciples urge Jesus to send this woman away, but she insisted that Jesus would heal her daughter. There are times when people around you will discourage and distract you from seeking after God but keep on praying for your miracle, there will be times when people will give you the wrong advice and cause you to step away from his presence. But you have to understand that he said in his word that I will never leave you nor forsake you even to the end.

This woman press forward and keep pushing until she receive a word from Jesus. Matthew 15:28 says ***"Then Jesus answered and said to her, "O woman, great is you faith! Let it be to you as you desire." And her daughter was healed from that very hour."***

God has promised you your miracle and don't give up keep pushing. There are times when God is waiting on us so that he can release our miracle.

You must remember that you're never alone, he is always there with you. A young woman was led of God to move to a distant city to get a new job. When she announced her resignation at work, everyone told her how much they'd miss her. Then someone asked, "Do you have any family where you're going?"

"No," she said

"Do you have any friends there?"

"No"

"Do you mean you're going all by yourself?"

"No," the young woman said with a smile. "I never go anywhere alone. God will be with me."

God has promised, *I will never leave thee nor forsake thee* (Hebrews 13:5).

There are many times we feel like God has left us alone. That's not true. We are the ones that walk away from God. When God created the heaven and earth he created man in his own likeness and image. And then place them in a place where he can come and meet with them. The bible says that God made Adam and then Eve and gave them dominion over the earth. And in the cool of the day he will come down and sup with them. But one day Eve subjected herself to Satan and believes what he (satan) told her and she shared it with her husband and they both believed him. Read Genesis chapter two. After subjecting to satan and eat out of the tree of life they left the place where God has put them and went into hiding. When God came down as usual in the cool of the day he could not find Adam and Eve, because they went into hiding, hiding from God.

Whenever martial problems, financial problems, sickness or other situations comes your way the devil wants to tell you that God has forgotten you that's not true its because we have left the place and gone into hiding. But again the bible says "he will never leave you nor forsake you to the very end." It's time to check yourself and see where God has placed you and also check to see if you have left that place where he expected you to be. There are times when God sent us to our knees and he came to find us on our knees but we are not there. Be at the place where GOD expects to meet you. Your miracle is there at the place where God tells you to be. If God says meet me every Friday into fasting and prayer just do what he says. Disobedience caused Adam and Eve to drift away from God's presence. They were a shamed of themselves, they saw themselves naked. So always keep this with you that God will never leave you unless you leave him.

Let me remind you of the famous poem "One set of footprints in the Sand." God said "when you look and saw that one set of footprints it wasn't yours it was mine, because when you got tired I picked you up and was carrying you in my arms."

How can God release my miracle?

There was a time in my life when it seemed like hell was let loose on me. Everything was happening the wrong way with me. There was so much attack from the enemy that at one time I started to question my salvation. So I decided to go into fasting and prayer seeking God for answers. It was midnight one Saturday night while praying with some other believers the Lord spoke to me and told me to read Exodus chapter 14:13-14.

"Moses answered the people, "Do not be afraid. Stand firm and you will see the deliverance the LORD will bring you today. The Egyptians you see today you will never see again. The LORD will fight for you; you need only to be still."

After reading this scripture I realized that I was trying to fight my own battle to gain victory which would be my miracle. But I then recognized from that scripture that the only way and time God will release my miracle is; if I would stand still and don't fight in my own strength. But to seek him and let him fight for me. The bible says not by might nor by power but by my Spirit says the Lord. One of the things I personally learn in life is that God doesn't struggle like we struggle.

The bible says Seek ye first the kingdom of God and his righteousness and all these things shall be added unto you. What will be added to you? Your healing, your deliverance, your financial breakthrough, your miracle but the most important thing you must do, so that he can release your miracle is that you must serve him whole heartily and faithfully.

Serving God whole heartedly and faithfully is one of the most important things in our lives that will release our miracle. 1 John 3:23 says *And whatsoever we ask, we receive of him, because we keep his commandments, and do those things that are pleasing in his sight.*

There are five things that every Christians should activate in their lives so that God can release their miracles and also their anointing.

- Activate a lifestyle of worship
- Activate prayerful lifestyle
- Activate the word of God. Be hearers and doers of his word
- Activate a lifestyle of Faith
- Activate a lifestyle of holiness and righteousness

When you activate these areas in your life you will realize that the anointing of God will help you to receive your miracle and your victory. And your miracle will be released. It doesn't matter what is your sickness or situation, you will be released from every yoke and bondage.

The bible says the true anointing breaks the yoke.

God promised you a miracle and you should realize that God never fails from his promise ever. Man fails on what they promise but God never did. He promised to send a savior to the world who died on the old rugged cross for our sins and shame, who was wounded for our transgression, who was bruised for our iniquity, the chastisement of our peace was upon him and who took stripes on his back for our healing. He promised us a comforter who is the Holy Spirit. Today we have the Holy Spirit who dwells within us.

For God to release your miracle you must keep looking up unto him. The bible says in Hebrews 12:2 ***Looking unto Jesus, the author and finisher of our faith; who for the joy that was set before Him endureth the cross, despising the shame, and is set down at the right hand of the throne of God."***

One of the things that will happens when we look up unto Jesus the author and finisher of our faith; is that he will release our miracle in such a supernatural way that we cannot comprehend. God has given gifts according to his will and that is because he wants to bring his promise to fulfillment.

God promised Gifts and one of the gifts he promised is the gift of healing. Why did he promise the gift of healing, it is because he wants to heal his people. So he gave the gifts of healing to those that he chooses so that the gift of healing can be in operation in the church.

You must remember as a Christian there are gifts that has been given just to benefit you as a believer in Christ. Stand on the promises of God. He will give you your miracle. There may be times when you feel that your miracle is so far away from coming but keep in mind that the bible says They that wait upon the Lord shall renew their strength.

So often, we don't reach out to receive what God has promised us because we think, I'm not a very good

Christian. The problem is that condemnation will keep us from acting on our faith. Many Christians have faith to receive a promise, but they won't act on it because of condemnation.

Condemnation is a faith killer. It will make us fear and draw back from the promises of God. We might know we have authority in Jesus' Name to rebuke cancer or some other disease, but we will put up with it instead because we know we've failed. We may say. "I am healed!" when we're around our Christian friends, but in our hearts we aren't really expecting healing to happen because the enemy is continuously reminding us of our mistakes.

Jesus paid the price for our sins so we could be clean and free. Even if we've blown it. 1 John 1:9 says, if we confess our sins, he is faithful and just to forgive us our sins, and to cleanse us from all unrighteousness. I've had people say to me, "You don't know what I've done," And I answer them, "And you don't know how powerful the blood of Jesus is." No matter what you may have done, when you ask God for forgiveness, the blood of Jesus cleanses you so that it's as though you'd never sinned.

Romans 8:1 SAYS, There is therefore now no condemnation to them which are in Christ Jesus. When your faith is unhindered by condemnation, you can act on your faith to receive everything God has promised you in His Word.

God never fails from his promise. He always fulfills his promise so keep holding on and never let go. In the book of Hebrews 10:23 he says *"Let us hold fast the profession of our faith without wavering; for he is faithful that promised;"*

CHAPTER THREE

HINDRANCES THAT CAN BLOCK YOUR MIRACLE

"Examine yourselves as to whether you are in the faith. Test yourselves. Do you not know yourselves that Jesus Christ is in you? unless indeed you are disqualified."
11 Corinthians 13:5

If ever you are believing God for a miracle and it seems that the miracle is not happening; then you need to check for the hindrances. There are several things that can cause hindrances in your life and cause you to lose or delay your miracle or breakthrough.

Your question may be "Well how do I know if there's a hindrance in my life or what should I do to get rid of it?" The answer is simple 'PRAYER." The bible says in the book of 1 John 5:14-*15 "And this is the confidence that we have in him, that if we ask any thing according to his will, he heareth us: And if we know that he hear us, whatsoever we ask, we know that we have the petitions that we desired of him."* And the only way you can get rid of these hindrances is to stay focused on God, he will help us to get rid of hindrances and stumbling blocks from our lives.

All of us face difficult situations at times that can easily distract us from what we're called to do for God. I was facing a distracting situation one day, and I thought, Lord I don't know if I can do this. But God told me, "Yes you can." Then He began to speak to me about staying focused. He said, "But you must stay focused on Me to be able to do what I have asked you to do."

How do you stay focused on God? You abide in Him through His Word. Jesus told His disciples. "If you will abide in Me, I will abide in you." (see John 15:4). Abiding in God means developing a relationship with Him through prayer, the Holy Spirit, and studying His Word.

Jesus went on to say, "If you abide in Me, and My words abide in you, you will ask what you desire, and it shall be done for you." (see John 15:7). That's basically what the Lord was saying to me. "Stay focused on Me. Speak what I speak. Do what I do. Then you become a magnet that draws everything to your need." And the distraction of the enemy will not able to penetrate in you.

Staying focused on God and abiding in Him are choices that you make. It's a matter of deciding. Okay, I'm going to stay focused. God's Word says *"I can do all things through Christ who strengths me."* Philippians 4:13. When the Word of God is your foundation, you can go to the Word before your difficulties become distractions so that you stay focused on God.

I have found that it takes no more effort to focus on God's Word than it does to focus on worry. In fact, focusing on God is a lot easier because when you get into worry, you become anxious. The "what ifs" start, and your mind begins to race. But peace comes when you focus on God's Word. You can relax and say, "God's Word is truth, and it's working in my life."

One day a woman came in my office and said Pastor I have given my life to Jesus Christ in one of your miracle service and the reason I give my life to the Lord is because I received a miracle. So I said what did the Lord do for you? She said he heals from twelve years of migraine headache. But I have one problem and that is I have been trusting God for a miracle that I will have a good relation with my family and I did everything in my power to get back this good relationship with my family but it's not happening. She said Pastor I am doing everything you said for me to do. I love the Lord, I am praying every morning, I am giving donations to the church but yet this one miracle that I am waiting for will not happen.

The first thing I thought about was to pray with her. So I ask her to join me in prayer. While praying the Lord spoke to me and said "Son why are you praying for a miracle? Let her deal with the spirit of unforgiveness and stop focusing on the problem and start focus on me and my Word. And the Lord spoke to me to share a scripture with her. Immediately I stop praying and started to counsel her and read Matthew 5:44-45 which says ***"But I say unto you, Love your enemies, bless them that curse you, do good to them that hate you, and pray for them which despitefully use you, and persecute you; That ye may be the children of your Father which is in heaven: for he maketh his sun to rise on the evil and on the good, and sendeth rain on the just and on the unjust."*** At that moment she confessed to the Lord that she did have a spirit of unforgiveness and that she was only focusing on the family dysfunction and not on his word and promises. She said "But I don't know how to get rid of it".

I take her to the word of God and let her know the promises of God and then led her in prayer. Now she is having a good relationship with her family and God has been moving mightily in their lives. Glory be to God.

In the past year or so, the Holy Spirit has been showing me the importance of learning to forgive those who harm us or cause us pain and grief. There are numerous passages in the bible where Jesus teaches about the importance of forgiving others. Unforgiveness can hinder our miracle.

In Matthew 6:14-14, Jesus says, ***"For if you forgive men when they sin against you, your heavenly Father will also forgive you. But if you do not forgive men their sins, your Father will not forgive your sins."***

In Chapter eighteen of Matthew, Jesus tells the parable of the servant who was forgiven a large debt. Soon after the king forgave him, he accosted a fellow servant and demanded to be repaid what the other man owed him. When the king found out that the first servant refused to show compassion on his fellow servants, the king placed all of his original debt back on him.

In this manner, harboring a spirit of unforgiveness is very dangerous and detrimental to us. When we choose to forgive others, it allows God to work a miracle for us. Asking for forgiveness is very important. Especially asking forgiveness for our own sins, and then forgiving others, we gain healing for ourselves. Our miracles can be easily released by releasing yourself from the spirit of unforgiveness.

Learning this principle earned this woman her victory with her family. In the book of Ephesians 4:26-27, Paul tells us, ***"In your anger don not sin: Do not let the sun go down while you are still angry, and do not give the devil a foothold."*** Satan will use a spirit of unforgiveness to hold us bondage, if we let him. Quite often these days, this type of bondage is perpetrated on children, who don't know any better. Satan then uses these hurts and abuses, suffered at a tender age, to keep us imprisoned for the rest of our lives. Now, however, the truth is out, and the truth can set you free. For God to release your miracle, learn to forgive others, for God showed mercy to all through the death of Jesus; we can do no less.

Many Christians want their miracle but don't want to get rid of their hindrances and stumbling blocks. Hindrances and stumbling blocks is what will keep you away from your healing, financial breakthrough, your love relationship, your family togetherness, etc.

If you want to experience your miracle get rid of your stumbling blocks and hindrances, and if you want to know how to get rid of the them examine yourselves as the scripture says in 2 Corinthians 13:5

God still do miracles but many people are not receiving their miracles because of the hindrances that kept them in captivity. Many Christians are suffering with so many hindrances that they don't know if the promises of God is still available to them.

There are so many hindrances that can be blocking your miracles: You are about to receive your miracle if only you can identify your hindrances and stumbling blocks and then allow God to work the miracle for you.

Some of the hindrances and stumbling blocks are:

Unforgiveness – causes bitterness and resentment. The spirit of unforgivenss ties your heart and put you into captivity. You need to untie that knot from your heart. As a Christian and a follower of Jesus Christ, we have that authority. Jesus said, *"I will give you the keys of the* *kingdom of heaven and whatever you bind on earth will be bound in heaven, and whatever you loose on earth will be loosed in heaven."* Matthew 16:19. You have the power to bind every spirit of unforgiveness and release yourself from it. Unforgiveness is one of satan's tool to attack people from getting their miracle and breakthrough. Mark 11:25-26 says *"And when ye stand praying, forgive, if ye have ought against any: that your Father also which is in heaven may forgive you your trespasses. But if ye do not forgive, neither will your Father which is in heaven forgive your trespasses."*

Compromise – The bible says that King Saul disobey God and tried to do his own thing. 1 Samuel 10:8 And thou shalt go down before me to Gilgal; and behold, I will come down unto thee, to offer burnt offering, and to sacrifice sacrifices of peace offerings: seven days shalt thou tarry, till I come to thee, and shew thee what thou shalt do.

One of the things that we must learn to never disobey God's commands or instructions in order to solve our own problems. Many times we as Christians are taking advice from the people who don't know God or people who profess that they know God and are compromising by doing things that God hates. The scripture says in the book of Samuel, *"What has thou done? And Saul said, because I saw that the people were scattered from me, and that thou camest not within the days appointed, and that the Philistines gathered themselves together at Mishmash; Therefore said I, the Philistine will come down now upon me to Gulag, and I have not made supplication unto the Lord; I forced myself there fore, and offered a burnt offering. And Samuel said to Saul, Thou has done foolishly: thou has not kept the commandment of the Lord thy God, which he commanded thee: for now would the Lord have established thy kingdom upon Israel for ever. But now thy kingdom shall not continue: the Lord hath sought him a man after his own heart, and the Lord hath commanded him to be captain over his people, because thou hast not kept that which the Lord commanded thee."* 1 Samuel 13:11-14.

We have to learn that incomplete obedience is disobedience. God is looking for those who have perfect hearts toward Him. The bible says the eyes of the Lord run to and fro throughout the whole earth to shew himself strong in behalf of them whose heart is perfect toward him. Rebellion is like the sin of witchcraft.

There is one character in the bible that we all should take as an example in our lives. Job was a man who suffered, and lost every thing that he had but he refused to compromise and subject himself to any satanic authority but stayed focus on God. Job had his wife and friends who discourage him and who was his stumbling block, but yet the bible says Job response to all of his suffering was "Thou he slay me yet will I serve him"

Job did not let hindrance or stumbling blocks keep him away from God. He knew what God has promised. He knew that God will bring him through. No other book in the bible answers the problem of human suffering like the book of Job. There are three things about Job that I believe we should know to give us hope when we are sick or waiting for a miracle from God.

Three things we should know about Job.

First, Job dwelt within God's hedge of divine protection. Because God protected Job, his home, and his property, satan hated him. Satan wanted job to compromise. He sneered, *"Does Job fear God for nothing?"* Job 1:9, insinuating that Job loved God only because He blessed him.

Second, Job's afflictions were from satan. When God healed Job, the Bible says that He turned the captivity of Job. Job 42:10. When you think of afflictions captivity, you can better understand Peter's statement in Acts 10:38. How God anointed Jesus with the Holy Spirit and with power: who went about doing good and healing all that were oppressed (or in captivity) of the devil.

Third, Job's faith was simple. Rather than suppress his feelings over what satan had done to him or charge God with any wrong doing, Job opened his soul to God and expressed his deepest feelings. He said, Though He (God) slay me, yet will I trust Him. Job 13:15.

The story of Job holds out hope to you who is feeling the sting of affliction and loss. Despite everything that happened to him, Job trusted God; and because he did, God blessed the end of his life more than the beginning. Job 42:12.

You must understand that satan's purpose is to derail every Christian from the destiny that God has put them on. His main purpose is to steal, kill and destroy while the purpose of God is to give Life and Life more abundantly. Satan wants to distract us from every promise that God has given us. So the only way he (satan) can accomplish that plan is to bring hindrances and stumbling blocks to us, causing us to sin against God.

Take a close look at Job and learn from his experience. The bible tells us that God restored Job's health, wealth and everything else that he had that is because he stayed focused on God, and refused to comprise. You must keep in mind of one thing and that is, God never cause sickness. He is a healer, a deliverer and a miracle worker. Keep standing on his promises. Miracle still Happens.

CHAPTER FOUR

HOW TO RECEIVE YOUR MIRACLE

"For with God nothing shall be impossible."
Luke 1:37

Receiving your miracle is very simple. The first thing we should do is to check our walk with God and secondly make sure we are living our life according to his word and not to disobey his word.

There was a time in my life when I used to be living from pay check to pay check. My walk with God was perfect. I attended church regularly, I fasted and prayed regularly, and I did everything that seems right. But yet I was struggling financially.

One day I decided to go before God to seek answer on how to receive a miracle. As I was praying the Holy Spirit help me to understand one thing and that is to follow God's principle and worship him. That's simple, by doing so it will release your miracle.

One of the things that I personally learn is that prayer is great and it moves the hand of God but worship move the heart of God and as you follow God's principle and worship him he will work a miracle for you.

David was called a man after God's own heart. Why? Because he worshiped the Lord in his spare time, and even during working. What about the woman whose daughter was vex with a spirit and came to Jesus for her daughter's healing. Jesus breaks the rule to fulfill this woman's request. Why? Because she worshipped and plead to him for his mercy. Jesus said, ask and it shall be given unto you, seek and you shall find and knock and it shall be open unto you.

Worship helps to release God's principles in your life. Some of God's principles are as follows:

- Live a life Faith
- Live a life without comprise
- Live a life of Holiness
- Live a life that is pleasing to God
- Live a God fearing life.
- Live a life of Worship
- Seek him diligently

Following the principles of God is simple. You must understand that God is your source. And he is able.

The book of Luke says *"And he said, the things which are impossible with men are possible with God."* Luke 18:27. Also the bible says *"And Jesus said unto them, Because of your unbelief; for verily I say unto you, If ye have faith as a grain of mustard seed, ye shall say unto this mountain, remove hence to yonder place; and it shall remove; and nothing shall be impossible unto you. Howbeit this kind goeth not out but by prayer and fasting."* Matthew 17:20-21.

God is an awesome and mighty God! He has everything in control even though it seems that everything around you is out of control! There are times that God seems a million miles away, but in reality, He is closer than we think.

He is as close as the mention of His name! Whatever your needs may be, He is always there to help bear our load. If we are tempted, He is able to deliver. If we are sick, He is able to heal. And whenever we need a miracle, God is till the miracle worker!

Our miracle has been promised by God himself. Psalms 23 has a promise that was given to us.

The 23rd Psalm

The Lord is my shepherd;
I shall not want.
He maketh me to lie down in green pastures;
He leadeth me beside the still waters.
He restoreth my soul;
He leadeth me in the paths of righteousness
For his name sake;
Yea, though I walk through
The valley of the shadow of death,
I will fear no evil;
For thou art with me;
Thy staff they comfort me.
Thou preparest a table before me
in the presence of mine enemies;
thou anointest my head with oil;
my cup runneth over.
Surely goodness and mercy shall follow me
all the days of my life;
And I will dwell in the house of the LORD for ever.

I do not want, in any way, to portray our Saviour as some kind of errand boy who is at our beckon and call. But, I do want to say that God is concerned about His children, and He is always there to answer the prayer that is ushered out of a heart of faith!

It seems that many times the reason why people fail to receive a miracle from God is not because they have not prayed. It is not because they have not known God's will or Way. But, it was because of lack of faith and the living of God's principle.

God is an Awesome and Mighty God and is able to perform a miracle for you!

There is no lack to our God and His mighty power. He is not some gray-headed grandfatherly figment of our imagination that walks stooped over with some weather beaten staff in his hand.

The God of the bible is an Almighty God who knows no limitations or bounds. He is the Ancient of Days who fills up all space and time! He is the Great Creator of this universe who has made all things including man whom He made in His own image.

And what God becomes to us strictly depends upon how we really see Him. How big He becomes depends on how we put the magnifying scope of His Word to our spiritual eyes, and focus in upon a God who is bigger than anything we could ever imagine.

In the book of Romans 10:17 the bible says "faith cometh by hearing, and hearing by the word of God."

God is not a Struggling God and He doesn't want his people to be struggling!

God showed Moses in His Deliverance of Israel that He was Mightier than Pharaoh and his armies! He showed Joshua that He was still bigger than the walls of Jericho and every barrier to victory. He showed Jehoshaphat that some battles don't belong to man, but that they belong to God.

In the New Testament, after man had not heard from God for four hundred years because of sin's separating power, angels heralded the arrival of a Deliverer and a Savior. And the Jehovah God who had so often delivered in man's past stepped out of the shadows of eternity in time and came again to show us that God is certainly more than enough for our every need.

He opened blinded eyes, unstopped deafened ears, caused the dumb to speak, the lame to leap, and the dead to rise again.

Luke 4:18-19 says *"The Sprit of the Lord is upon me, because he hath anointed me to preach the gospel to the poor; he hath sent me to heal the brokenhearted, to preach deliverance to the captives, and recovering of sight to the blind, to set at liberty them that are bruised, to preach the acceptable year of the Lord."*

God is the ruler over everything!
He has created everything.

Your miracle is very simple to receive. God rules the Heavens. In the book of Isaiah 66:1 says "Thus saith the LORD, the heaven is my thorne, and the earth is my footstool: where is the house that ye build unto me? And where is the place of my rest?

He rules the earth. In the book of Psalms 24:1 says "The earth is the Lord's and the fullness thereof; the world, and they that dwell therein.

God is!
- A peace Speaker and the problem solver
- The miracle worker and the heart mender
- My provider and my supplier
- My shepherd and my song
- My sword and my shield
- The Healer of all my diseases, the forgiver of all my iniquities.
- He is Holy and highly exalted
- Merciful and he is majestic, there is nothing too hard for Him.
  There is no miracle that He cannot do! He is the creator of the universe.
- A God that provide physically, emotionally, financially or spiritually

The bible says that God is a rewarder of them that diligently seek him. There is no sickness that He cannot cure!
- Aids or Alzheimer's
- Arthritis or anorexia
- Bulimia or bursitis
- Cataracts or cancer
- Depression or diabetes

Psalms 116:8-10 says "For thou hast delivered my soul form death, mine eyes from tears, and my feet from falling. I will walk before the Lord in the land of the living. I believed, therefore have I spoken……."

Job 10:11-12 says " Thou has clothed me with skin and flesh, and hast fenced me with bones and sinews. Thou has granted me life and favor, and Thy visitation hath preserved my Spirit."

1 Peter 3:12 says "For the eyes of the Lord are over the righteous, and His ears are open unto their prayers."

James 5:16 says "Confess your faults one to another, and pray one for another, that ye may be healed. The effectual fervent prayer of a righteous man availeth much."

Isaiah 43:2 says "When thou passest through the waters, I will be with thee; and through the rivers, they shall not overflow thee:......"

11 Corinthians 3:17 says "Where the Spirit of the Lord is, there is liberty."

Are you ready for a Miracle?
Then follow his principle, seek him diligently and obey his word. Remember the bible says seek ye first the kingdom of God and his righteousness and all these things shall be added unto you, meaning that it will automatically comes to you when you seek him.

Miracles, signs and wonders played a major role in the early church. The good news is; the days of miracles, signs and wonders are not over. The manifestation of the wonder working power of God accomplishes many things. His power is still demonstrated in our society.

You need to know God still does miracles. You have the right and responsibility to ask God for miracles. Our purpose for desiring God's wonder working power is not for any flesh to glory in His presence but for him to receive all glory and honor.

If God can heal the lame man then he can heal you. If God can perform miracles in Ephesus then he can do it for you. One of God's reasons for performing miracles is to confirm his Word.

Every time I go to preach I always seek God for signs wonders and miracles. Healing, deliverance, signs and wonders can happen any time any where. One thing is certain the wonder working power of God will always happen. All we need to do to receive it is to pray earnestly and have faith.

CHAPTER FIVE

GOD HAS THE POWER TO HEAL AND CHANGE THINGS

Christ hath redeemed us from the curse of the law, being made a curse for us: for it is written, Cursed is every one that hangeth on a tree: That the blessing of Abraham might come on the Gentiles through Jesus Christ; that we might receive the promise of the Spirit through faith.
Galatians 3:13-14

Have you ever been at a place in your life where you felt as if something had to change? Bartimaeus was a man in the Bible who felt that way (see Mark 10:46-52). He was a blind man who sat on the side of the road every day, begging for alms, an outcast of society. Then someone told Bartimaeus about Jesus, and suddenly he realized that he didn't have to be blind anymore. He made up his mind that it was time for a change.

One day he heard a great commotion coming towards him on the highway. He must have asked someone what was happening, and they told him, "Jesus of Nazareth is coming this way," because Bartimaeus began to cry out, "Jesus, Son of David, have mercy on me!"

When Jesus heard the blind man's desperate cry, He stopped in His tracks, and said, "Bring the blind man to me." Bartimaeus flung aside his beggar's robe, scrambled to his feet, and hurried to the Master.

Jesus asked Bartimaeus, "What do you want Me to do for you? And he exclaimed, "Lord, I want to receive my sight! I want to see!"

"Your faith has made you whole," the Lord replied, and instantly the blind man could see!

I would like to assure you that God still does these kinds of miracle until this day. He still hears and attends to every heart that cries out his name. Are you ready for a dramatic change in your life? Jesus has the power to change things for you just as He did for Bartimaeus. He is coming your way. He waits only to hear your cry of faith.

When you face a troubling situation, you must take action. Stand on the promises of God. Go to him. Tell your heavenly Father your problem, because He knows all about it, and He has a way for you to survive. Survival is not an ugly word. Survival causes you to overcome, which can take you to a place of total victory. And that's where God wants you to be.

Jesus said "Greater works than these shall ye do…" Jesus has power to change things. Some say miracles have ceased. But if Jesus says greater works than these shall ye do then it means that we have the authority to change things.

Jesus' foreknowledge and perception of the end-time was very revealing. He said "He that believeth on me, the works that I do shall he do also; and greater works than these shall he do; because I go unto my Father," John

14:12. He saw the body of Christ doing greater works than He had done. That is very interesting. More miracles! More devils cast out! More dead raised! And even more sick healed.

Jesus says "For verily I say unto you, That whosoever shall say unto this mountain, Be thou removed, and be thou cast into the sea; and shall not doubt in his heart, but shall believe that those things which he said shall come to pass; he shall have whatsoever he saith." "Therefore I say unto you, What things soever ye desire, when ye pray, believe that ye receive them, and ye shall have them!" Mark 11:23-24.

You see the Spirit of God Brings Life. If the Spirit of him that raised up Jesus from the dead dwell in you, he that raised up Christ from the dead shall also quicken your mortal bodies by his Spirit that dewlleth in you. Romans 8:11

The very same Spirit that raised Christ from the dead dwells in you! Jesus was beaten beyond recognition, crucified, and left in the tomb for three days. He was beyond all natural hope, yet the Spirit raised Him back to life!

Today you may find yourself facing circumstances that are beyond all natural hope, but the same Spirit that raised a Jesus from the dead is that same Spirit dwells in you! And the Scripture says that He doesn't just live in you; He's there to quicken or - make alive - everything in your life.

Are you felling like all hope is gone and there is no hope? Is your spiritual life dead in the inside? You need to be quickened and brought back to life? God can change that situation or work that Miracle. He is a miracle worker.

If you have dead finances, the Spirit of God can quicken them. If you're struggling in you marriage, your family, or your physical body, the same Spirit that quickened Jesus can quicken whatever is broken in you! Apply the Word of God in your life. He has your promises in his Word. Expect your miracle.

God sent Jesus to the Cross to die for us, and then He left us this assurance the same Spirit which delivered Jesus from the dead is placed inside each and every one of us. Everything it took to raise Jesus from the grave dwells inside of us to quicken our situation and bring it back to life.

He went to the cross for you. He did go to the cross he couldn't help himself. No he went to the cross that you may have peace, healing and forgiveness of sin.

You have to remember that God has power to change things. He gave us the opportunity to let loose our self from bondage. Jesus said ***"And I will give unto thee the keys of the kingdom of heaven: and whatsoever thou shalt bind on earth shall be bound in heaven: and whatsoever thou shalt loose on earth shall be loosed in heaven."*** Matthew 18:18. God has vested in you the power to bind and loose. Grab hold of what he has promised you and allow the changing power to change your situation and circumstances.

One day a woman came up to me and said "Pastor I have a situation and that is every time I look at the scars that is on my skin it takes me back to the days when I was being abused by my husband. So can God really work a miracle and change this situation for me." My answer to her was "give God the glory for his delivering power which has delivered you from that abuse." And oh of course YES, YES, YES he has the power to change things and every situation that brings bad memories. And secondly I told her that she needs to use those scars as a testimony to other and also for herself to remind her of who God really is. I then also reminded her about Jesus. Was it not for the scars in Jesus' hands and sides how could he have proven to Thomas that he is the risen Christ.

John 20:27 says *"Then said he to Thomas, reach hither thy finger, and behold my hands, and reach hither thy hand, and thrust it into my side and be not faithless but believing."* Also the book of Galatians 6:17 says, *"From henceforth let no man trouble me for I bear in my body the marks of the Lord Jesus."*

This situation had shaped this women's life, filled her with fear and distrust and hidden inside of her was a wonderfully talented individual who has the ability to do the work of the Lord.

We all have scars of some kind. I have one on my left pinky finger from childhood. Scars are an inevitable part of life. Scars are the way life writes stories into our flesh. Some people try to hide their scars and are successful, but you can't hide the pain that came with the scar like this woman. The reason for this is because some scars are physical and some are emotional and some are spiritual. A great part of my ministry is spent listening to people talk about their scars and their pain. But in spite of all I can tell you that there is a God who can be touched by the feeling of our infirmities and change every situation and scares from worst to better, more sadness to joy. There are times when you may think that he don't know what you are facing much less to change it but take note that God knows what you're going through and he has the power to change it for the good.

You may have scars from physical abuse or mental abuse; you may be wounded spiritually; you may be hurt in the past, but the purpose of this book is to let you know

Jesus has scars too but his scars were there to remind us that he has the power to heal and change things. Jesus is a wounded healer and has the authority to change things. It takes somebody who has been wounded to help heal another wounded person. So look at your scars as a tool to help someone that is going through what you have gone through.

There are times when things will or may happen to you that will change you. But always remember that God has the power to use those situations to bring a change in your life. There will be times when our wounds, hurt and scars will remind us at times of our pain, but our scars identify who we are. Always remember that you don't see Christ fully unless you see his scars. And you need to know that seeing your scars doesn't mean that you are defeated because Jesus scars was not a sign of defeat but victory.

One person asked me once if my scars ever remind me of my past. Oh sure it does remind me of something but definitely not my past. It reminds me of my victory and the many times I defeat the devil in the past in Jesus Name.

You have to realize one thing here; there is power in your scars. Let me ask a simple question here. Have you ever felt like God has turned his back on you? Well the answer is not really he just want to show you the stripes on his back just to remind you of what he has done for you. Have you ever felt like God is throwing his hands up at you? Well he is showing you the scars of your healing. That is where the power is, the healing it's in the scars and wounds of our savior and Christ.

He is the Lamb slain from the foundation of the World he is a God with scars and stripes and is willing to change your situation with perfect examples. In revelations chapter 5 when John saw the book and no one was worthy to open it one of the elders said weep not the root of David hath prevailed to open the book and John looked and saw a Lamb as it had been slain. The wound scarred Christ. There are times when you must know that your scars and stripes are powerful.

Take your scars and rejoice for he will use your scars to change your situation. God doesn't just help us get over our pain he changed the very pain into joy and testimony.

CHAPTER SIX

MIRACLE THROUGH FAITH

Verily I say unto you, If ye have faith, and doubt not, ye shall not only do that which was done to the fig tree, but also if ye shall say unto this mountain, Be thou removed …. It shall be done.
Matthew 21:21

What is faith – Faith a belief in or confident attitude toward God, involving commitment to His will for one's life. The bible says "Now faith is a substance of things hoped for, the evidence of things not seen."

Every Christian should know that God promised a blessing. And we need to understand that we should hope for the very things that God promised us even though we are not seeing it at the very moment.

God promises are as follows:
- Healing from sickness
- Deliverance from oppression and depression
- Deliverance from Demonic spirits
- Blessings financial, Spiritually, Emotionally, Physically

- Salvation
- Peace

I can continue to list so many things that God has promised us. And every promise can be provided to us miraculously. But how can I receive that which he promised me. The answer is simple and that is FAITH.

The bible says *"Let us hold fast the profession of our faith without wavering: for he is faithful that promised; every promise in the word of God."* Hebrew 10:23

Every one of us is expecting great things to happen to us in life. We want every good thing in life. But there is a price for everything. One of the most important things we need to know is that God still do miracles, but there is something that God required from us so that we can receive from him and that is faith. And what measure of faith, the bible says just have faith as little as a mustard seed. If you have faith as little as a mustard seed it can remove mountains of troubles and problems out of your life.

Every Christian needs to understand that you can only receive the miraculous by faith. The bible says "Now the just shall live by faith: but if any man draws back, my soul shall have no pleasure in him." Hebrew 11:1

What the scripture is saying is that every one should have faith. By having faith we are going to receive that which is promised to us.

The faith of little Gabriella.

I love to share this miraculous healing that took place on a Wednesday night Bible study just because of the faith of a little child. Gabriella was seven years old and had allergic reactions. Her sickness was much wearied.

Gabriella was allergic to any thing that is made out of wheat flour. It was very sad that she could not enjoy the food that many other kids enjoyed. She could not eat anything like cookies, pizza, chicken nuggets, just to name a few. Her mother was very much grieving especially when she eats something that Gabriella couldn't eat.

There are times when she would ask her mother and sister how the cookies tasted. This would grieve them so much. But she had faith that God would heal her.

One Wednesday night her mother brought her to our regular Bible Study. It was a normal night but Gabriella's faith had risen up within her soul. She walked up to me and said "Pastor please pray for me, so that I can eat whatever I see my friends would eat." I felt very sad to hear this child request.

I laid my hands on her and called for a cookie. I gave her the cookie to eat and believed God together with her faith, that God will heal her. The next day when Gabriella went to school she requested a cup cake for lunch. Her teacher who knew she could not eat anything with flour told her that she could not give her a cup cake because she was informed by the parent about her allergic reactions.

Gabriella's faith arose so high she said to her teacher "Miss I was healed in the church service last night." Her faith brings her healing. To this day Gabriella is eating anything she chooses to eat and she is no longer suffering from any form of allergic reactions anymore. Glory be to God.

Do you have faith like this little child? I believe God places faith in our hearts, and He wants to help us fulfill them. Do you have faith in your heart that has almost died because something happened that devastated you? No matter what has happened in your past, don't loose hope. God can give that Faith back to you.

Maybe you feel that you've failed him and he wouldn't help you to gain faith again. I know how that feels because I have experienced that before. But God specializes in mending broken faith, healing wounded hearts, and making something beautiful out of our lives.

Maybe you have a history of making bad decisions and you think God could never forgive you. I believe with all of my heart and I speak with the confidence of knowing God's word that there is nothing you could have done that God cannot and will not forgive.

You simply have to ask him. ***"If we confess our sins, He is faithful and just to forgive us our sins."*** 1 John 1:9

However, God cannot forgive you if you don't ask him. That is where your faith will start to restore. God has done His part by making forgiveness available to you through Jesus Christ. Now you have to do your part and reach out to receive that forgiveness.

You may want to pour your heart out to Him or simply pray a few words from your heart. I know of people who did not receive their miracle because they failed to believe God to restore them of their faith. God can erase your past failures and help you fulfill your hearts desire as you trust in him. But you have to do this by faith.

The bible says "That the communication of thy faith may become effectual by the acknowledging of every good thing which is in you in Christ Jesus."

If ever you are going to receive your breakthrough, you have to have faith. There are times when we as Christian need to let go and let God do it for us. Notice in the story of blind Bartimaeus that he cast off his beggar's robe before he received his miracle. (see Mark 10:50). In those days a beggar wore a garment that represented his station in life. It was a beggar's robe, and it symbolized everything that was wrong in his life. When Bartimaeus took off his beggar's robe, he was saying, "I'm casting off my old life. I'm wiping the slate clean."

When you're believing God for a miracle, it's important for you to cast off your "beggar robe." Your old way of thinking can keep you from receiving what you needed from God. It not about how you know to get it. It's all about your faith in God.

If ever you want to receive that which was promised to you, the first thing you need to do is to please God. But you may ask the questions how can, I please God. The answer is very simple and that is Faith.

The bible says "But without faith it is impossible to please him: for he that cometh to God must believe that He is, and that He is a rewarder of them that diligently seek Him."

Faith is very important. It is very simple to receive God's supernatural miracles in your life. You don't have to do any rituals, ceremony or need any special prayer. Your faith is what matters. To please God you must have faith and if you have faith it will please Him, because he is your only source.

The book of Isaiah chapter sixty give us some ways we can step up to a new level of faith.
1. Expect a new supply – Isaiah 60:6
2. Expect to live in the favor of God – Isaiah 60:10
3. Expect the gates of provision to come open and stay open – Isaiah 60:11

Faith to receive your miracle

When you read John chapter five, we find people bound by infirmities; these individuals were blind, halt, withered, and impotent. And was lying by a pool where an angel of the Lord would come and visit once a year. At that pool there was one man who was there for 38 years with a disease waiting for someone to help him get into the water when the angel comes.

As he was waiting one day Jesus came to the scene and healed him. This day was not just another day for this man. This day was a day, where he put his faith in Jesus and requested his healing, so Jesus saw and felt the anguish and hurt of this man and had compassion. He felt the man's disappointment and was moved to help him.

Jesus is a miracle worker and would desire to make your day different than what it is. This day is not like no other. If you are in need, and have faith you have a miracle ready to happen. If you have an infirmity in your body, and have faith, you have a miracle ready to happen.

Why don't you step out in faith away from the crowd, away from your peers, forget about what others may think, call on the name of the Lord Jesus and receiver your miracle today by faith. MIRACLES STILL HAPPEN.

Let this be not just another day, but let this be your day for a miracle. Luke 11:9-10 says " Ask and it shall be given unto you, seek and you shall find, knock and it shall be opened unto you. For every one that asketh receiveth; and he that seeketh findeth; and to him that knocketh it shall be opened".

CHAPTER SEVEN

MIRACLE THOUGH THE WORD

This book of the law shall not depart out of thy mouth; but thou shalt meditate therein day and night, that thou mayest observe to do according to all that is written therein: for then thou shalt make thy way prosperous, and then thou shalt have good success.
Joshua 1:8

Word of God – the means by which God makes Himself known, declares His will, and brings about His purposes. Phrases such as "word of God" and "word of the Lord" are applied to the commanding word of God that brought creation into existence (Genesis 1; 2 Peter 3:5) and also destroyed that same world through the waters of the Flood (2 Peter3:6); to God's announcement of an impending or future act of judgement (Exodus 9:20-21); to the word that declares God's commitment and promises. His blessing (Gen. 15:1, 4) and to a particular instruction from God (Joshua 8; 27).

The word of God is very important in our lives. Every promise about our healing and miracle is in the word of God. The bible says *"And keep the charge of the Lord thy God, to walk in his ways, to keep his statutes, and his commandments, and his judgments, and his testimonies, as it is written in the law of Moses, that thou mayest prosper in all that thou doest, and whitersoever thou turnest thyself."* 1 Kings 2:3.

The Bible is God's revealed Word, but it's also a book about human beings crying out to God in the struggles of life. What does the Bible tell us to do to get our miracle? He promises to work wonders for us. One thing it says is to wait upon the Lord.

In Isaiah 40:31 it says, *"They that wait upon the Lord shall renew their strength; they shall mount up with wings as eagles".* Used in this verse, "wait upon the Lord" refers to renewing and strengthening. It also implies waiting for the answer, much like a farmer waits for his seeds to germinate after he plants them. He cannot make them grow. All he can do is plant them and then wait for God to bring forth the harvest.

There are times in our lives when we seek God for a miracle but we have not patience to wait upon God. That is why it is very important to know the word of God.

When we study the word of God it will teach us patience and help us to walk right into our miracle. The prophet Elijah had to wait upon the Lord after he prayed for rain to come upon the parched earth of Israel (see 1 Kings 18:41-44). Initially he prayed that it would not rain until the people turned from their evil ways. In answer to that prayer, God withheld rain for over three years. It was a bitter experience for the children of Israel, but one that brought them to their knees.

If ever we are going to experience the fullness of God's promises of miracle in our lives we need to know the word of God. Memorizing and meditating on scriptures. The purpose of memorizing the word is that it teaches us the superiority of God's wisdom.

The word of God builds in us an excitement and expectation of the miraculous results of applying scripture in our everyday lives. The bible says *"For if ye shall diligently keep all these commandments which I command you, to do them. To love the Lord your God, to walk in all his ways, and to cleave unto him; then will the Lord drive out all these nations from before you, and ye shall possess greater nations and mightier than yourselves. Every place whereon the soles of your feet shall tread shall be yours: from the wilderness and Lebanon, from the river, the river Euphrates, even unto the uttermost sea shall your coast be. There shall no man be able to stand before you; for the Lord your God shall lay the fear of you and the dread of you upon all the land that ye shall tread upon, as he hath said unto you."* Deuteronomy 11:22-25.

Millions of Christians today are suffering and are loosing their blessing because they don't know what God has promised them, because they are not reading and mediating upon the Word of the Lord.

Let's take a look at some biblical characters that meditate and know the Word.

David: The man after God's own heart - The bible says, "O how love I thy law! It is my mediation all the day. Thou through thy commandments hast made me wiser that mine enemies: for they are ever with me. I have more understanding than all my teachers: for thy testimonies is my mediation. I understand more that the ancients, because I keep thy precepts. (Psalm 119:97-100). The word of God meant every thing to David. David was able to slay his giant, not in his own strength but in the strength of Lord. Why? Because he knew what was the promises of God. He knew the Word of God.

Joshua: The leader - The bible says, *"Only be thou strong and very courageous, that thou mayest observe to do according to all the law, which Moses my servant commanded thee: turn not from it; to the right hand or to the left, that thou mayest prosper whithersoever thou goest. This book of the law shall not depart out of thy mouth: but thus shalt mediate therein day and night, that thou mayest observe to do according to all that is written therein: for then thou shalt make thy way prosperous, and then thou shalt have good success."* Joshua 1:7-10.

Joshua was commanded by God to meditate upon the word, his (God) Word. The fulfillment of prosperity could have only come to Joshua because he knew the word of God. And he was very obedient to the Word.

Stephen: The Martyr – The bible says *"And Stephen, full of faith and power, did great wonders and miracles among the people."* Acts 6:8.

It was the power of the Word. The bible says *"In the beginning was the word and the word was with God and the word was God."* John 1:1. Knowing the word, is knowing the miracle worker (Jesus).

The Word of God is so important in our lives. How will you know what is promised to you if you don't read the Bible. There are so many benefits of knowing the Word of God.

You can receive your miracle through the Word of God; by knowing the word of God you will succeed at everything you do. You will also experience the supernatural blessing, healing, deliverance and favor of God upon your lives. See Psalm 128.

One of the most important miracles you will receive by knowing the word of God is your lives will be transformed according to 11 Corinthians 5:17. When you mediate upon the Word, God will speak to you personally about your situation, problems and desires of your hearts. See Psalm 37:4.

When a believer in Christ read the Bibles and mediate upon it they will experience the miraculous result of applying God's wisdom to their lives. James 1:5 says *"If any of you lack wisdom, let him ask of God, that giveth to all men liberally, and upbraideth not; and it shall be given him."*

One of the things that the Word of God does to us is that it cleanses us from false philosophies, wrong affections, beliefs, word and actions. See Psalm 19:7. The Word of God will cause you to grow and increase in your spiritual capacity and help you to walk right into your miracle.

Another thing you need to know is that when you believe the Word, miracles happen. One day when Jesus was in the city of Cana, a nobleman from Capernaum went to see Him. (See John 4:46-54). The nobleman's son was at home, deathly ill, and he begged the Lord to come and heal his child. Instead of going with him, Jesus asked, "Won't any of you believe in me unless I do more and more miracles?" Ignoring the question, the nobleman pleaded with Him, "Sir, please come now before my child dies."

Jesus saw that the man had faith, and He also knew there was no distance in prayer. He said, "Go back home. Your son is healed!" And the man believed Jesus and started home.

When Jesus' word is mixed with faith, it can cause a miracle to move faster than the speed of light to where you are. Look what happened. The nobleman knew that his son's life was hanging in the balance. Everything hinged upon whether or not he believed the Lord. He believed the words of Jesus, and he turned around and started home.

Before he got there, some of his servants met him with the news that his son had recovered! He asked them when the boy had started to feel better, and they replied, "Yesterday afternoon at about one o'clock his fever suddenly disappeared! (v.52). That was the exact moment when Jesus had told him, "Your son is healed." Just like that father, when you choose to believe the words of Jesus no matter what we see, miracles can happen in our lives!

Our miracle is in the Word. The reason many people are not receiving their miracle is because there are times when they don't understand something, they want to ignore it. But we can't ignore the Holy Spirit or look away from the Word because the Holy Spirit and the Word is the source of God's power in our lives. God declared in Zechariah 4:6 that His power flows not by might, nor by power, but by my spirit. The power of God doesn't come into our lives by intelligence or by human ability. It's by the Holy Spirit.

In Genesis 1:1, 2 it was God who spoke the words that created the earth and the Holy Spirit who moved upon the face of the waters and transformed chaos into beauty. And throughout the Bible, it was the Holy Spirit who came upon the prophets and anointed them to speak the Word of God and do what He commanded. And the wonderful thing is we can know the word of God and the Holy Spirit personally.

Mediating upon scripture day and night is the only activity which God guaranteed will cause you to succeed in every thing you attempt. Matthew 6:33 says "Seek ye first the kingdom of God, and his righteousness; and all these things shall be added unto you.

This is because the Word is inspired of God, according to 11 Timothy 3:16-17. Jesus said sitting at His feet and hearing His word must be the number one priority in our lives. (See Luke 10:38-42). Because God speaks to us by his Spirit through His Word, His word the Bible says became flesh and dwell among men.

For you to experience God's miraculous power in your life you must fill your lives with God's Word and follow such lifestyle with worship. His Word will lead you to your miracle. Following God's instruction which is his WORD is very important. Unless you read and understand his instruction you will not able to experience an easy flow of success towards your miracle.

I was traveling in a plane once where I had experienced a situation that can really make any one feel bad if they don't read instructions. It was snack time during the flight when the hostess handed out peanuts. The gentleman that was sitting next to me was struggling with the pack of peanuts trying to open it. So while he was struggling with the pack of peanut, I opened my pack of peanuts and was eating. After he tried over and over again he then asked "How did you opened your pack of peanut so simple and I am having a hard time opening mine." I said to him "sir look at the top of the pack it says PLEASE TEAR HERE." It's that simple. Read the instruction.

The bible is God's basic instructions. If ever you're going to receive your miracle then you must mediate and depend upon the word of God.

CHAPTER EIGHT

MIRALCE OF FINANCIAL BLESSINGS

―⊙※―

"The blessing of the LORD, it maketh rich, and he addeth no sorrow with it."
Proverbs 10:22.

There are lots of people who have their heart set on getting rich. The mistake made usually lays both in the nature of the thing they desire and in the way by which they hope to get it.

The most desirable kind of wealth is not just having abundance, but having it with no sorrow mixed in. Most rich people are very anxious about their wealth. They worry about many things, such as the best way to invest it, how to keep it, how to get more, and they have a fear of losing it or having it stolen. Likewise, the misuse of riches can bring guilt and may ruin ones health through excessive eating and drinking.

The Apostle Paul warns about what happens to those who desire to be rich.

The bible says "But those who desire to be rich fall into temptation and a snare, and into many foolish and harmful lusts which drown men in destruction and perdition. For the love of money is a root of all kinds of evil, for which some have strayed from the faith in their greediness, and pierced themselves through with many sorrows. 1 Timothy 6:9-10

When you are asking God for riches let them be a source of comfort to your soul. You must plan to do good with them and to serve God with joyfulness and gladness of heart in the use of them. You want to be clean rich, not filthy rich!

That kind of wealth is desirable, and it can be expected, not by making ourselves slaves to the world, but by the blessing of God. That kind of blessing, which comes into your lives from the love of God and has the grace of God for its companion, is to be desired. No sorrow or grief is in God's package deal. He gives us richly all things to enjoy;

Other comments about riches are made earlier in the tenth chapter of Proverbs. The wicked and the righteous are contrasted in verses two and three. Proverbs 10:2-5 says "Treasures of wickedness profit nothing: but righteousness delivereth from death. The LORD will not suffer the soul of the righteous to famish: but he casteth away the substance of the wicked.

In verse 4-5 let us know that, even though we should consider riches without sorrow as a blessing from the Lord, we still must be diligent and wise, rather than be slipshod or lazy. "He becometh poor that dealeth with a slack hand:

but the hand of the diligent maketh rich. He that gathereth in summer is a wise son: but he that sleepeth in harvest is a son that causeth shame.

I want to remind you that God enjoys bestowing blessing upon his children. He delights in giving good gifts to his people.

He is ready, willing and anxious to add blessing after blessing to our lives. In fact, the Lord looks upon us as the apple of his eye. As deeply concerned and as carefully attentive as man can be for the safety of his eyesight, so is God for the protection and welfare of his people. We are his most precious possession.

How many of you choose to do something special for your family? The greatest joy I have found in life is to do good things for those I love. It's a pleasure! God take pleasure in doing good for his people.

God is our living heavenly Father and he longs to bless you. He looks for ways to bestow favor upon you. He enjoys enriching your life, just like he did with his friend, Abraham.

The bibles says in Genesis 12:1-3 "Now the LORD had said unto Abram, Get thee out of thy country, and from thy kindred, and from thy father's house, unto a land that I will shew thee: And I will make of thee a great nation, and I will bless thee, and make thy name great; and thou shalt be a blessing: And I will bless them that bless thee, and curse him that curseth thee: and in thee shall all families of the earth be blessed."

He blesses some people more that others simply because he knows they will be a blessing to others.

The Lord had blessed Abraham in all things. Read what one of Abraham's servants said to the household of Laban in Genesis 24:34-36.

After Hannah, who had been childless throughout her marriage, prayed to the Lord for a child and he heard her cry and gave her a son, she weaned him and then brought the child Samuel to the temple, where she loaned him to the LORD in a selfless act of loving dedication.

In her prayer of praise, thanksgiving and rejoicing, Hannah said: 1 Samuel 2:7-8 "The LORD maketh poor, and maketh rich: he bringeth low, and lifted up. He raiseth up the poor out of the dust, and lifted up the beggar from the dunghill, to set them among princes, and to make them inherit the throne of glory;"

No matter how much blessings you have, the supply of his treasure house will never be diminished. God wants you to have blessings. That blessing comes when you get a revelation of his loving kindness toward you, when you have a passion for him to bless you, and when you actively pursue and seek his blessing. The bible says ask and it shall be given upon you, with good measure press down, shaken, and running over.

The author of the Hebrews speaks of Esau as being a profane man, who for one morsel of meat sold his birthright. Then the apostle Paul makes this comment, For ye know how that afterward, when he would have inherited the blessing, he was rejected; for he found not place of repentance, though he sough it carefully with tears.

Those are certainly sad words. The inspired word tells us there in Hebrew 12 that Esau was both a fornicator and a profane man. His profanity was his contemptuous treatment of his birthright – that which should have been held sacred and invaluable. It was the selling of position, honour, influence, power, pre-eminence, for a dish of soup. It was the parting with being the next in line to be head of the clan at the bidding of an empty stomach. It was the allowing of the sensual to swallow up the spiritual. It was sinking the interest of a great future in the little pressing need of the present.

Esau would have inherited the blessing, but he didn't. Jacob got the blessing with no sweat. His father gave it to him as an inheritance. Passion and pursuit did that for him.

Take a look at Joshua 24. Joshua Inherit a blessing. I want you to see that the blessing of the Lord is something we simply inherit because of a covenant he made with our forefathers in the faith. The bible says "Abraham I will bless them that bless you, and curse them that curse you."

Joshua declared that God's people would enjoy the blessings of the land of Canaan, even though they had not sewn the crops, built the cities, nor planted the olive trees. The gospel of John, Jesus promised that a spiritual realm of blessings would be given to his people, even though they had done nothing to deserve it. They would reap a bountiful harvest of souls where they had not even sown the gospel seed. An abundant crop and a goodly inheritance would be given them.

Long before Joshua's day as is seen in Genesis 28:3-4 Isaac said to his son, Jacob, whose name was later changed to Israel: And God Almighty bless thee, and make thee fruitful, and multiply thee, that thou mayest be a multitude of people; And give thee the blessing of Abraham, to thee, and to thy seed with thee; that thou mayest inherit the land wherein thou art a stranger, which God gave unto Abraham.

In the book of Matthew 25:34 it says ***"Then shall the King say unto them on his right hand, come, ye blessed of my Father, inherit the kingdom prepared for you from the foundation of the world:"***

Even as the descendants of Abraham, Isaac and Jacob eventually inherited the land of Canaan that God gave them, so do we, who are favored by the Lord the King, inherit the kingdom he prepared for us at the creation of the world. God has many precious blessings for us that we did not work to earn.

The Samaritan woman who came to Jacob's well had her mind set on drawing some cold, clear water out of the well with a bucket let down into its depths on a rope. Jesus, however, had the real thing in mind – the water of eternal life. He told her it was a gift – the Gift of God!

If you think you are good enough to receive the miracle of Blessing, you are wrong. Chronic seekers of the miracle of Blessings seek to earn the blessing of the Lord. The bible seek ye first the kingdom of God and his righteousness and then all these things shall be added unto you.

When Jesus told his disciples, "I have meat to eat and to finish his word, they thought he was speaking of natural food, but Jesus spoke of real food, which is doing God's will.

God's kingdom is not carnal; it is spiritual. It is not meat and drink; it is righteousness, peace and joy in the Holy Ghost. You inherit it, just as surely as Israel was to inherit the Land of Canaan. But if you doubt, like Israel in the wilderness, you will come short of his promise.

In order for an heir to enjoy the benefit of his inheritance, he must do something. He must believe the report and then lay claim to the inheritance. Every year, vast amounts of estates and huge sums of money sit unclaimed in state and federal banks and are held in escrow by courts because those to whom the property or money should go did not show up to collect it. In some cases, they were unable to be notified. In other instances, those who could have been heirs doubted the authenticity of the notification letter they received.

Under Moses' leadership, the Israelites doubted that God would give them the land of Canaan for a possession. Their reasoning was that they could not take the land because many of its inhabitants were giants. They were right; they could not – but could! So because of their negative attitude, God excluded them.

After serving a forty years probation, during which most of the unbelievers died, the younger generation presumed to capture the city of Ai in their own power, despite the fact that God said they would be defeated. They made the same error their fathers had made. They thought they could do it in their own power. In both instances, they disregarded the word of God.

They might have said, "Well, since it was wrong for our parents to doubt they could defeat the giants, we will go in without fear. We can do it, no matter what Joshua tells us about waiting on the Lord.

What they forgot was that conquering Ai had nothing to do with their strength or military prowess. Their sin was that of self-presumption. They imagined they could do it on their own.

It is like wise true today that efforts at self-salvation and self-blessing will ultimately fail. The Bible says. "The wages of sin is death, but the gift of God is eternal life through Jesus Christ." The Bible says in Ephesians 2:8-9 **"For by grace are ye saved through faith: and not of yourselves: it is the gift of God not of works, lease any man should boast."**

Whether it is fear of self-presumption, either can exclude us from the blessing of God. Only Faith gains the promises because whatsoever is not of faith is sin. God must receive all the glory!

It is commendable for a person to earn his own way through life in this world. The bible says a man ought not to eat if he does not work.

The bible says in Genesis 3:17-*19 "And unto Adam he said, Because thou hast hearkened unto the voice of thy wife, and hast eaten of the tree, of which I commanded thee, saying, thou shalt not eat of it: cursed is the ground for thy sake; in sorrow shalt thou eat of it all the days of thy life; Thorns also and thistles shall it bring forth to thee; and thou shalt eat the herb of the field; In the sweat of thy face shalt thou eat bread, till thou return unto the ground; for out of it wast thou taken; for dust thou art, and unto dust shalt thou return."*

In the delightful garden of Eden, the vigorous and productive soil yielded a spontaneous produce, and the industry of man was confined to the easy and pleasant work of checking or regulating the luxuriant growth of vegetation. Life would have gone on this way forever for Adam and his wife had it not been for their disobedience to God's word.

The profuse growth of thorns and thistles was a part of the curse that fell on man when he sinned. His sorrow would be a result of the labor and sweat he would have to expend to get the soil to produce the food necessary for survival. Instead of the spontaneous and luxuriant fruits of the garden, the herb of the field, which required diligent cultivation, was from now on to provide a principal part of his diet.

Man sentenced to a lifetime of hard labor; he was sentenced to die. Death, in its full meaning, is the cutting off, not merely of existence, but of life, and life includes all the gratifying experiences of which we are humanly capable. Death is the cutting off of all the sources of human enjoyment, and among them of the physical life itself.

Jesus, in speaking to his disciples at the well in Sychar (Shechem), told them. "my meat is to do the will of him that send me, and to finish his work." He would work, so we could enjoy the fruit of his labor. He would build, so we could inherit. He would conquer, so we could be overcomers.

Luke 22:44 *"And being in an agony he prayed more earnestly: and his sweat was as it were great drops of blood falling down to the ground."*

The ground, which had been cursed by the LORD because of man's transgression, and would henceforth bring forth fruit only by hard labor and sweat, was blessed to feel the touch of Jesus' sweat. Because he labored in prayer, one day the earth itself will be restored to its pristine glory of an Eden-like condition.

You see, the blessing of the Lord has nothing to do with neither our efforts nor our worthiness. We do not earn God's love; we do not merit the mercy of God; rather, we **inherit** these things.

Deuteronomy 7:6-8 "For thou art an holy people unto the LORD thy God; the LORD thy God hath chosen thee to be a special people unto himself, above all people that are upon the face of the earth. The LORD did not set his love upon you, nor choose you, because ye were more in number than any people; for ye were the fewest of all people: But because the LORD loved you, and because he would keep the oath which he had sworn unto your fathers, hath the LORD brought you out with a might hand, and redeemed you out of the house of bondmen, from the hand of Pharaoh king of Egypt."

Joshua told the Israelites the same thing: Joshua 24:13-14 I have given you a land for which you did not labor, and cities which you did not build, and you dwell in them; you eat of the vineyards and olive groves which you did not plant. Now therefore, fear the LORD, serve Him in sincerity and in truth, and put away the gods which your fathers served on the other side of the River and in Egypt, Serve the LORD!

We have a great example in Joshua: He declared that everyone under his roof would serve God. You can be the kind of priest of your homes God wants you to be. Just stand up and serve God acceptable, with reverence and godly fear. Be strong in the Lord. You will inherit the kingdom blessings!

It was at Schechem that the cursing and blessings were spoken to Israel on mounts Ebal and Gerizim.

To be blessed and inherit the blessings, they had to obey God's word. The result of disobeying His word would be to live under as curse. It's interesting that when the curse was pronounced that would come as a result of their disobedience, all Israel was commanded to say "Amen". No encouragement to affirm their agreement was necessary, however, when the blessings were mentioned!

If you would like to enjoy the miracle of blessings from the Lord, all you need to do is to love him and serve him. Adam only lost the blessing of God and fell under a curse that added much sorrow to his life when he chose to go his own way rather than obey God's word.

The Israelites did the same thing. And Israel was removed from their God-given inheritance into Babylon when they rejected the Word of the Lord in the mouth of his prophets and chose the way of a carnal, fleshly lifestyle.

Those who obey the Word of God will inherit the kingdom. It yours God has promise to bless you. Just love and obey him, cling to him and do His will. All is prepared for you. You can enjoy the miracle of blessings. You can inherit the blessings because it was promised to you.

CHAPTER NINE

MIRACLE OF DELIVERANCE

*"If the Son therefore shall make you free,
ye shall be free indeed"*
John 8:36

Heal the sick, cleanse the lepers, raise the dead, cast out devils: freely ye have received, freely give.
Matthew 10:28

Writing this book is a battle. The devils hate being exposed. But I thank my personal Lord and Savior Jesus Christ daily for his many blessing, strengths and breakthrough in my life. And I know that God will release your miracle of deliverance by the time you started to apply some of the principles I mention in this book.

How to know when people need the Miracle of Deliverance!

It is very simple to know when someone needs a miracle of deliverance. First of all when someone is sick and doctors cannot diagnose their sickness or disease they definitely need a miracle of deliverance. Because when a person is possessed with a demonic spirit medical science cannot detect it.

It is very simple of a person to received deliverance from oppression, depression or demonic spirits. The bible says ***"Verily, Verily, I say unto you, He that believeth on me, the works that I do shall he do also; and greater works than these shall he do; because I go unto my Father".*** John 14:12

This is the authority we have in Christ. We have been given the authority to cast out devils. Castings out demons are called deliverance. Deliverance is very much important. When a person is being tormented by a demonic spirit, medication or counseling cannot free them. A spiritual problem can only be solved by spiritual warfare. Matthew 17:20-21 says ***"And Jesus said unto them, Because of your unbelief: for verily I say unto you, If ye have faith as a grain of mustard seed, ye shall say unto this mountain, Remove hence to yonder place; and it shall remove; and nothing shall be impossible unto you. Howbeit this kind goeth not out but buy prayer and fasting."***

The Miracle of deliverance will restore confidence in the name of Jesus and his power. The bible tells us that whatsoever ye shall ask in my name, that will I do, that the Father may be glorified in the Son. John 14:13

The delivering power of Jesus Christ can deliver people from years of heartache, torment and sorrow. Many people are possessed with spirits and don't even know. Many times they think that they have some sort of medical problems. They go to doctors and sometimes witch doctors for help.

Let's take a look at what the bible says about demonic spirits. The bible describe the devil as:

Our adversary – 1 Peter 5:8 *"Be sober, be vigilant; because your adversary the devil, as a roaring lion, walketh about, seeking whom he may devour:"* The devil is our adversary; he wants to destroy God perfect creation. That is why the bible teaches us to be sober and be very vigilant.

Wicked – 1 John 2:14 *"I have written unto you, fathers, because ye have known him that is from the beginning. I have written unto you, young men, because ye are strong, and the word of God abideth in you, and ye have overcome the wicked one."*

In spite of Satan's attack and wickedness God has given each and every one of his people the authority over him. The bible says resist the devil and he will flee from us. We have the authority over demons, sickness and diseases. Jesus gave us that authority.

Then Jesus came to them and said, "All authority in heaven and on earth has been given to me. Matthew 28:18

And he said to him, "I will give you all their authority and splendor, for it has been given to me, and I can give it to anyone I want to. Luke 4:6

"And his fame went throughout all Syria: and they brought unto him all sick people that were taken with divers diseases and torments, and those which were possessed with devils, and those which were lunatic, and those that had the palsy; and he healed them." Matthew 4:24.

A major part of Jesus ministry involved the casting out of Devils. Matthew says *"And his fame went throughout all Syria: and they brought unto him all sick people that were taken with divers diseases and torments, and those which were possessed with devils, and those which were lunatic, and those that had the palsy; and he healed them."* Matthew 4:24.

Jesus gave his disciples authority over devils. The bible says that Jesus called his disciples together and gave them power. Luke 9:1 *"Then he called his twelve disciples together, and gave them power and authority over all devils, and to cure diseases."* This is one out of the hundreds of promised Jesus have given us.

Matthew 10:**8** *"Heal the sick, cleanse the lepers, raise the dead, cast out devils: freely ye have received, freely give."* The bible tells us that the disciples cast out many devils. And they cast out many devils, and anointed with oil many that were sick, and healed them. Mark 6:13. Jesus also gave the next seventy powers over devils. Luke 10:17 *"And the seventy returned again with joy, saying, Lord even the devils are subject unto us through thy name."*

Jesus says all power has been given unto you. You have the permission from Jesus himself to lay hand on the sick and pray in his name. You also have powers to cast out devils in his name. Luke 10:20 says *"Notwithstanding in this rejoice not, that the spirits are subject unto you; but rather rejoice because your names are written in heaven."* We should not be proud that we have powers over devils. But give him the glory for his deliverance power in our lives. And rejoice that we are saved and can bring others to him through his deliverance power. So always remember you have authority over devils. Mark 16:17-18 says *"And these signs shall follow them that believe; In my name shall they cast out devils; they shall speak with new tongues; They shall take up serpents; and if they drink any deadly things, it shall not hurt them; they shall lay hands on the sick, and they shall recover."*

Let me take you to the Bible where Deliverance occurs!

- David played on his harp to chase demons away. 1 Samuel 16:23
- A dumb spirit. Matthew 9:33
- The man's son. Matthew 17:18-21
- Man in the synagogue. Mark 1:25-26
- The demonic. Matthew 8:28
- Syrophenician woman's daughter. Mark 7:29-30
- Woman who followed Jesus. Luke 8:2-3
- A woman who had a spirit of infirmity. Luke 13:11-12
- Multitude vexed. Acts 5:16
- Philip. Acts 8:6-7
- The damsel. Acts 16:16-19
- Handkerchiefs. Acts 19:12
- Seven sons of Sceva. Acts 19:13-16

Even though we have powers over devils, we need to be very careful. We must be prepared, so we are not among the deceived. It is very important for us to be aware that seducing spirits are just as active today as they were when Jesus walked this earth.

Luke 21:8 says *"And he said, Take heed that ye be not deceived: for many shall come in my name, saying, I am Christ; and the time draweth near; go ye not therefore after them."*

1 Timothy 4:16 says *"Take heed unto thyself, and unto the doctrine; continue in them: for in doing this thou shalt both save thyself, and them that hear thee."*

In the final time, just before Jesus comes, we find that spirits of the devil will also be doing miracle. We need to be very careful. Revelation 16:14 says For they are the spirits of devils, working miracles, which go forth unto the kings of the earth and of the whole world, to gather them to the battle of that great day of God Almighty.

Being possessed by a demon can be very frustrating and discouraging. It can take a lot from you. There will be time when discouragement and hopelessness step in and you will feel like quitting. The devil will try to stop you and even try to kill you. You must let the devil know that you are not about to "give up" or "give in," no matter what he tries to send you way. God promised to deliver those that are oppressed and possessed, your miracle of deliverance was promised from the word of God. Never think of quitting especially when the enemy started to speak negatively to you.

The word 'quit' must not be in your vocabulary. Hopefully, somewhere along our road towards freedom, we'll get tired of the devil; so instead of him torment us, we'll decide to turn things around and tormenting him. You may face many setbacks and lose some of the battles along the way, but you must continue to fight as long as you have breath left in your body. The word of God says those that are with you are more than those that are against you! So rejoice.

Let's determine to fill our lives with God's Word, praise and worship and all those things we know will drive the devil crazy. We could call this a warfare mentality. You need to keep your lives filled with those things that will keep your relationship with Jesus at the center of your lives. Jesus must remain your number one priority at all times.

We have the authority in Christ!

In the bible God teaches us that we both have the authority and we are to use it Consider the teaching in Ephesians 6:10-18. Here we are told to put on the full armor of God it states that we wrestle not against flesh and blood but against the rulers, against the authorities, against the powers of this dark world and against the spiritual forces of evil in the heavenly realms.

To receive a miracle of deliverance you should do the following:
1. Make your requests known unto God. Treat God for who He is. He is not a puppet He is not there to do our bidding. You should not try and manipulate the Power of God. He is there and He will answer our request. After all He is God and He knows what is best for us simply ask Him to lead you and protect you in this battle. To lead you in what you say and do. That your words will be His words and His words your words.
2. Get into spiritual warfare. Command the spirits or sickness, firmly and confidently to go. You don't need to be afraid. The bible says at the name of Jesus every knee shall bow and every tongue shall confess that Jesus Christ is Lord.
3. Use the scriptures. Read out the portions of scripture where we are given authority. For example Luke 9:1-2; Luke 10:1, 17-20; Mark 16:17.

Use your authority that Jesus Christ has given you. Use the power that God has invested in you and let the Holy Spirit direct you. The bible says do not be afraid for lo I am with you all ways even unto the ends of the earth.

In the back of this book you will find a prayer for total deliverance. Pray that prayer and believe God for you deliverance.

CHAPTER TEN

Miracles of the Old Testament

—⁓◎⁓—

This chapter is taken from the word of God. God did great miracles in the days of old. And you are about to read some of it. The same God that did these miracles is still doing miracle today. Read of some of the wonderful miracle God perform in the days of the Old Testament.

The Miracle of the Nile River
Exodus 7:14-22

14 Then the LORD said to Moses, "Pharaoh's heart is unyielding; he refuses to let the people go. 15 Go to Pharaoh in the morning as he goes out to the water. Wait on the bank of the Nile to meet him, and take in your hand the staff that was changed into a snake. 16 Then say to him, 'The LORD, the God of the Hebrews, has sent me to say to you: Let my people go, so that they may worship me in the desert. But until now you have not listened. 17 This is what the LORD says: By this you will know that I am the LORD: With the staff that is in my hand I will strike the water of the Nile, and it will be changed into blood. 18

The fish in the Nile will die, and the river will stink; the Egyptians will not be able to drink its water."

19 The LORD said to Moses, "Tell Aaron, 'Take your staff and stretch out your hand over the waters of Egypt—over the streams and canals, over the ponds and all the reservoirs'-and they will turn to blood. Blood will be everywhere in Egypt, even in the wooden buckets and stone jars."

20 Moses and Aaron did just as the LORD had commanded. He raised his staff in the presence of Pharaoh and his officials and struck the water of the Nile, and all the water was changed into blood. 21 The fish in the Nile died, and the river smelled so bad that the Egyptians could not drink its water. Blood was everywhere in Egypt.

22 But the Egyptian magicians did the same things by their secret arts, and Pharaoh's heart became hard; he would not listen to Moses and Aaron, just as the LORD had said. 23 Instead, he turned and went into his palace, and did not take even this to heart. 24 And all the Egyptians dug along the Nile to get drinking water, because they could not drink the water of the river.

The miracle of Marah's Healing Waters
Exodus 15:22-27

22 Then Moses led Israel from the Red Sea and they went into the Desert of Shur. For three days they traveled in the desert without finding water. 23 When they came to Marah, they could not drink its water because it was bitter. (That is why the place is called Marah). 24 So the people grumbled against Moses, saying, "What are we to drink?" 25 Then Moses cried out to the LORD, and the LORD showed him a piece of wood. He threw it into the water,

and the water became sweet. There the LORD made a decree and a law for them, and there he tested them. 26 He said, "If you listen carefully to the voice of the LORD your God and do what is right in his eyes, if you pay attention to his commands and keep all his decrees, I will not bring on you any of the diseases I brought on the Egyptians, for I am the LORD, who heals you." 27 Then they came to Elim, where there were twelve springs and seventy palm trees, and they camped there near the water.

The Miracle of Miriam's Leprosy

Numbers 12:1-16

1 Miriam and Aaron began to talk against Moses because of his Cushite wife, for he had married a Cushite. 2 "Has the LORD spoken only through Moses?" they asked. "Hasn't he also spoken through us?" And the LORD heard this. 3 (Now Moses was a very humble man, more humble than anyone else on the face of the earth.) 4 At once the LORD said to Moses, Aaron and Miriam, "Come out to the Tent of Meeting, all three of you." So the three of them came out. 5 Then the LORD came down in a pillar of cloud; he stood at the entrance to the Tent and summoned Aaron and Miriam. When both of them stepped forward, 6 he said, "Listen to my words: "When a prophet of the LORD is among you, I reveal myself to him in visions, I speak to him in dreams. 7 But this is not true of my servant Moses; he is faithful in all my house. 8 With him I speak face to face, clearly and not in riddles; he sees the form of the LORD. Why then were you not afraid to speak against my servant Moses?" 9 The anger of the LORD burned against them, and he left them. 10 When the cloud lifted from above the Tent, there stood Miriam—leprous, like snow. Aaron turned toward

her and saw that she had leprosy; 11 and he said to Moses, "Please, my lord, do not hold against us the sin we have so foolishly committed. 12 Do not let her be like a stillborn infant coming from its mother's womb with its flesh half eaten away." 13 So Moses cried out to the LORD, "O God, please heal her!" 14 The LORD replied to Moses, "If her father had spit in her face, would she not have been in disgrace for seven days? Confine her outside the camp for seven days; after that she can be brought back." 15 So Miriam was confined outside the camp for seven days, and the people did not move on till she was brought back. 16 After that, the people left Hazeroth and encamped in the Desert of Paran.

The Miracle of the Sun Standing Still
Joshua 10:12-15

12 On the day the LORD gave the Amorites over to Israel, Joshua said to the LORD in the presence of Israel: "O sun, stand still over Gibeon, O moon, over the Valley of Aijalon." 13 So the sun stood still, and the moon stopped, till the nation avenged itself on its enemies, as it is written in the Book of Jashar. The sun stopped in the middle of the sky and delayed going down about a full day. 14 There has never been a day like it before or since, a day when the LORD listened to a man. Surely the LORD was fighting for Israel! 15 Then Joshua returned with all Israel to the camp at Gilgal.

The Miracle of fire from heaven
11 Kings 1:9-15

9 Then he sent to Elijah a captain with his company of fifty men. The captain went up to Elijah, who was sitting on the top of a hill, and said to him, "Man of God, the king says, Come down! 10 Elijah answered the captain, "If I am a man of God, may fire come down from heaven and consume you and your fifty men!" Then fire fell from heaven and consumed the captain and his men. 11 At this the king sent to Elijah another captain with his fifty men. The captain said to him, "Man of God, this is what the king says, 'Come down at once!" 12 "If I am a man of God," Elijah replied, "may fire come down from heaven and consume you and your fifty men!" Then the fire of God fell from heaven and consumed him and his fifty men. 13 So the king sent a third captain with his fifty men. This third captain went up and fell on his knees before Elijah. "Man of God," he begged, "please have respect for my life and the lives of these fifty men, your servants! 14 See, fire has fallen from heaven and consumed the first two captains and all their men. But now have respect for my life!" 15 The angel of the LORD said to Elijah, "Go down with him; do not be afraid of him." So Elijah got up and went down with him to the king.

CHAPTER ELEVEN

Miracles of the New Testament

This chapter is taken from the word of God. God did great miracles in the days of old. And you are about to read some of it. The same God that did these miracles is still doing miracle today. Read of some of the wonderful miracle God perform in the days of the New Testament.

Jesus Changes Water to Wine
John 2:1-11

1On the third day a wedding took place at Cana in Galilee. Jesus' mother was there, 2and Jesus and his disciples had also been invited to the wedding. 3When the wine was gone, Jesus' mother said to him, "They have no more wine." 4"Dear woman, why do you involve me?" Jesus replied, "My time has not yet come." 5His mother said to the servants, "Do whatever he tells you." 6Nearby stood six stone water jars, the kind used by the Jews for ceremonial washing, each holding from twenty to thirty gallons. 7Jesus said to the servants, "Fill the jars with water"; so they filled them to the brim. 8Then he told them, "Now draw some out and take it to the master of the banquet." They did so, 9and the master of the banquet tasted the water that had been turned into wine. He did not realize where it had come from, though the servants who had drawn the water knew. Then he called the bridegroom aside 10and said, "Everyone brings out the choice wine first and then the cheaper wine after the guests have had too much to drink; but you have saved the best till now." 11This, the first of his miraculous signs, Jesus performed in Cana of Galilee. He thus revealed his glory, and his disciples put their faith in him.

The Miracle of the Nobleman's Son
John 4:46-54

46Once more he visited Cana in Galilee, where he had turned the water into wine. And there was a certain royal official whose son lay sick at Capernaum. 47When this man heard that Jesus had arrived in Galilee from Judea, he went to him and begged him to come and heal his son, who was close to death. 48"Unless you people see miraculous signs and wonders," Jesus told him, "you will never believe." 49The royal official said, "Sir, come down before my child dies." 50Jesus replied, "You may go. Your son will live." The man took Jesus at his word and departed. 51While he was still on the way, his servants met him with the news that his boy was living. 52When he inquired as to the time when his son got better, they said to him, "The fever left him yesterday at the seventh hour." 53Then the father realized that this was the exact time at which Jesus had said to him, "Your son will live." So he and all his household believed. 54This was the second miraculous sign that Jesus performed, having come from Judea to Galilee.

The Miracle of the Impotent Man
John 5:1-9

1Some time later, Jesus went up to Jerusalem for a feast of the Jews. 2Now there is in Jerusalem near the Sheep Gate a pool, which in Aramaic is called Bethesda[a] and which is surrounded by five covered colonnades. 3Here a great number of disabled people used to lie—the blind, the lame, the paralyzed.[b] 5One who was there had been an invalid for thirty-eight years. 6When Jesus saw him lying there and learned that he had been in this condition for a long time, he asked him, "Do you want to get well?" 7"Sir," the invalid replied, "I have no one to help me into the pool when the water is stirred. While I am trying to get in, someone else goes down ahead of me." 8Then Jesus said to him, "Get up! Pick up your mat and walk." 9At once the man was cured; he picked up his mat and walked. The day on which this took place was a Sabbath,

The Miracle of deliverance
Mark 1:21-27

21They went to Capernaum, and when the Sabbath came, Jesus went into the synagogue and began to teach. 22The people were amazed at his teaching, because he taught them as one who had authority, not as the teachers of the law. 23Just then a man in their synagogue who was possessed by an evil[a] spirit cried out, 24"What do you want with us, Jesus of Nazareth? Have you come to destroy us? I know who you are—the Holy One of God!" 25"Be quiet!" said Jesus sternly. "Come out of him!" 26The evil spirit shook the man violently and came out of him with a shriek. 27The people were all so amazed that they asked each other, "What is this? A new teaching—and with authority! He even gives orders to evil spirits and they obey him."

The Miracle of Provision
Luke 5:1-11

1One day as Jesus was standing by the Lake of Gennesaret, with the people crowding around him and listening to the word of God, 2he saw at the water's edge two boats, left there by the fishermen, who were washing their nets. 3He got into one of the boats, the one belonging to Simon, and asked him to put out a little from shore. Then he sat down and taught the people from the boat. 4When he had finished speaking, he said to Simon, "Put out into deep water, and let down the nets for a catch." 5Simon answered, "Master, we've worked hard all night and haven't caught anything. But because you say so, I will let down the nets." 6When they had done so, they caught such a large number of fish that their nets began to break. 7So they signaled their partners in the other boat to come and help them, and they came and filled both boats so full that they began to sink. 8When Simon Peter saw this, he fell at Jesus' knees and said, "Go away from me, Lord; I am a sinful man!" 9For he and all his companions were astonished at the catch of fish they had taken, 10and so were James and John, the sons of Zebedee, Simon's partners. Then Jesus said to Simon, "Don't be afraid; from now on you will catch men." 11So they pulled their boats up on shore, left everything and followed him.

The Miracle of Peter's Mother-in-law
Luke 4:38-40

38Jesus left the synagogue and went to the home of Simon. Now Simon's mother-in-law was suffering from a high fever, and they asked Jesus to help her. 39So he bent over her and rebuked the fever, and it left her. She got up at once and began to wait on them. 40When the sun was setting, the people brought to Jesus all who had various kinds of sickness, and laying his hands on each one, he healed them.

The Miracle of Mass Healing
Mark 1:32-34

32That evening after sunset the people brought to Jesus all the sick and demon-possessed. 33The whole town gathered at the door, 34and Jesus healed many who had various diseases. He also drove out many demons, but he would not let the demons speak because they knew who he was

The Miracle of the Leper Cleanse
Luke 5:12-15

12While Jesus was in one of the towns, a man came along who was covered with leprosy. When he saw Jesus, he fell with his face to the ground and begged him, "Lord, if you are willing, you can make me clean." 13Jesus reached out his hand and touched the man. "I am willing," he said. "Be clean!" And immediately the leprosy left him. 14Then Jesus ordered him, "Don't tell anyone, but go, show yourself to the priest and offer the sacrifices that Moses commanded for your cleansing, as a testimony to them." 15Yet the news about him spread all the more, so that crowds of people came to hear him and to be healed of their sicknesses.

The Miracle of the Paralytic
Luke 5:18-25

18Some men came carrying a paralytic on a mat and tried to take him into the house to lay him before Jesus. 19When they could not find a way to do this because of the crowd, they went up on the roof and lowered him on his mat through the tiles into the middle of the crowd, right in front of Jesus. 20When Jesus saw their faith, he said, "Friend, your sins are forgiven." 21The Pharisees and the teachers of the law began thinking to themselves, "Who is this fellow who speaks blasphemy? Who can forgive sins but God alone?" 22Jesus knew what they were thinking and asked, "Why are you thinking these things in your hearts? 23Which is easier: to say, 'Your sins are forgiven,' or to say, 'Get up and walk'? 24But that you may know that the Son of Man has authority on earth to forgive sins...." He said to the paralyzed man, "I tell you, get up, take your mat and go home." 25Immediately he stood up in front of them, took what he had been lying on and went home praising God.

The Miracle of the Withered Hand
Mark 3:1-6

1Another time he went into the synagogue, and a man with a shriveled hand was there. 2Some of them were looking for a reason to accuse Jesus, so they watched him closely to see if he would heal him on the Sabbath. 3Jesus said to the man with the shriveled hand, "Stand up in front of everyone." 4Then Jesus asked them, "Which is lawful on the Sabbath: to do good or to do evil, to save life or to kill?" But they remained silent. 5He looked around at them in anger and, deeply distressed at their stubborn hearts, said to the man, "Stretch out your hand." He stretched it out, and his hand was completely restored. 6Then the Pharisees went out and began to plot with the Herodians how they might kill Jesus.

The Miracle of the Centurion's Servant
Matthew 8:5-13

5When Jesus had entered Capernaum, a centurion came to him, asking for help. 6"Lord," he said, "my servant lies at home paralyzed and in terrible suffering." 7Jesus said to him, "I will go and heal him."

8 The centurion replied, "Lord, I do not deserve to have you come under my roof. But just say the word, and my servant will be healed. 9 For I myself am a man under authority, with soldiers under me. I tell this one, 'Go,' and he goes; and that one, 'Come,' and he comes. I say to my servant, 'Do this,' and he does it." 10 When Jesus heard this, he was astonished and said to those following him, "I tell you the truth, I have not found anyone in Israel with such great faith. 11 I say to you that many will come from the east and the west, and will take their places at the feast with Abraham, Isaac and Jacob in the kingdom of heaven. 12 But the subjects of the kingdom will be thrown outside, into the darkness, where there will be weeping and gnashing of teeth." 13 Then Jesus said to the centurion, "Go! It will be done just as you believed it would." And his servant was healed at that very hour.

The Miracle of the Widow's Son
Luke 7:11-18

11 Soon afterward, Jesus went to a town called Nain, and his disciples and a large crowd went along with him. 12 As he approached the town gate, a dead person was being carried out—the only son of his mother, and she was a widow. And a large crowd from the town was with her. 13 When the Lord saw her, his heart went out to her and he said, "Don't cry." 14Then he went up and touched the coffin, and those carrying it stood still. He said, "Young man, I say to you, get up!" 15The dead man sat up and began to talk, and Jesus gave him back to his mother. 16They were all filled with awe and praised God. "A great prophet has appeared among us," they said. "God has come to help his people." 17This news about Jesus spread throughout Judea[a] and the surrounding country.

The Miracle of the Stilling of the Storm
Matthew 8:23-27

23Then he got into the boat and his disciples followed him. 24Without warning, a furious storm came up on the lake, so that the waves swept over the boat. But Jesus was sleeping. 25The disciples went and woke him, saying, "Lord, save us! We're going to drown!" 26He replied, "You of little faith, why are you so afraid?" Then he got up and rebuked the winds and the waves, and it was completely calm.

27The men were amazed and asked, "What kind of man is this? Even the winds and the waves obey him!"

The Miracle of the Two Blind Man
Matthew 9:27-31

27As Jesus went on from there, two blind men followed him, calling out, "Have mercy on us, Son of David!" 28When he had gone indoors, the blind men came to him, and he asked them, "Do you believe that I am able to do this?" Yes, Lord," they replied. 29Then he touched their eyes and said, "According to your faith will it be done to you"; 30and their sight was restored. Jesus warned them sternly, "See that no one knows about this." 31But they went out and spread the news about him all over that region.

The Miracle of the Dumb Demonic
Matthew 9:32-35

32While they were going out, a man who was demon-possessed and could not talk was brought to Jesus. 33And when the demon was driven out, the man who had been mute spoke. The crowd was amazed and said, "Nothing like this has ever been seen in Israel." 34But the Pharisees said, "It is by the prince of demons that he drives out demons." 35Jesus went through all the towns and villages, teaching in their synagogues, preaching the good news of the kingdom and healing every disease and sickness.

The Miracle of Jairus' Daughter
Luke 8:41-58

41Then a man named Jairus, a ruler of the synagogue, came and fell at Jesus' feet, pleading with him to come to his house 42because his only daughter, a girl of about twelve, was dying. As Jesus was on his way, the crowds almost crushed him. 43And a woman was there who had been subject to bleeding for twelve years, but no one could heal her. 44She came up behind him and touched the edge of his cloak, and immediately her bleeding stopped. 45"Who touched me?" Jesus asked. When they all denied it, Peter said, "Master, the people are crowding and pressing against you." 46But Jesus said, "Someone touched me; I know that power has gone out from me." 47Then the woman, seeing that she could not go unnoticed, came trembling and fell at his feet. In the presence of all the people, she told why she had touched him and how she had been instantly healed. 48Then he said to her, "Daughter, your faith has healed you. Go in peace." 49While Jesus was still speaking, someone came from the house of Jairus, the synagogue ruler. "Your daughter is dead," he said. "Don't bother the teacher any more." 50Hearing this, Jesus said to Jairus, "Don't be afraid; just believe, and she will be healed."

51When he arrived at the house of Jairus, he did not let anyone go in with him except Peter, John and James, and the child's father and mother. 52Meanwhile, all the people were wailing and mourning for her. "Stop wailing," Jesus said. "She is not dead but asleep." 53They laughed at him, knowing that she was dead. 54But he took her by the hand and said, "My child, get up!" 55Her spirit returned, and at once she stood up. Then Jesus told them to give her something to eat. 56Her parents were astonished, but he ordered them not to tell anyone what had happened.

The Miracle of the Woman with an Issue of Blood
Matthew 9:20-22

20Just then a woman who had been subject to bleeding for twelve years came up behind him and touched the edge of his cloak. 21She said to herself, "If I only touch his cloak, I will be healed." 22Jesus turned and saw her. "Take heart, daughter," he said, "your faith has healed you." And the woman was healed from that moment.

The Miracle of the Deaf and Dumb Man of Decapolis
Mark 7:31-37

31Then Jesus left the vicinity of Tyre and went through Sidon, down to the Sea of Galilee and into the region of the Decapolis. 32There some people brought to him a man who was deaf and could hardly talk, and they begged him to place his hand on the man. 33After he took him aside, away from the crowd, Jesus put his fingers into the man's ears. Then he spit and touched the man's tongue. 34He looked up to heaven and with a deep sigh said to him, "Ephphatha!" (which means, "Be opened!"). 35At this, the man's ears were opened, his tongue was loosened and he began to speak plainly. 36Jesus commanded them not to tell anyone. But the more he did so, the more they kept talking about it. 37People were overwhelmed with amazement. "He has done everything well," they said. "He even makes the deaf hear and the mute speak."

CHAPTER TWELVE

DECLARATION

Miracles through Declaration

Declaration of Healing:
- I claim my healing in Jesus Name for the bible says he was wounded for my transgression and bruised for my iniquities, the chastisement of my peace was upon him and by his stripes I am healed.
- I know that I am free from every sickness and diseases in Jesus Name because the word says who the son of man set free is free indeed.
- I am healed and now become strong because the word says for the Lord is my tower and he gave me the power in Jesus name.
- Thank you Jesus for my healing from every sickness and diseases. I will continue to praise and worship you. Serving you all the days of my life. For you have been good to me.

Declaration of Deliverance:
- I am set free by the power of Jesus Christ and wash by the precious blood of Jesus Christ who died on the cross, buried and rose on the third day.
- I declare my freedom from every principalities and power from every demonic spirits in Jesus name.
- I am delivered from every demonic force that used to prevail against me.
- I wrestle against every principalities and power and ruler of darkness of wickedness in high places in Jesus Name.
- I declare power of every satanic power, for all powers have been given unto me to cast out devils in Jesus Name.

Declaration of Financial Blessings
- I am free from every debt and I declare my life debt free in Jesus Name.
- I am completely delivered from every financial curses from my past generation.
- I declare a financial blessing over my life and the lives of my families.
- I received my financial freedom in Jesus Name.
- I am blessed in Jesus Name in health, wealth and prosperity.

CHAPTER THIRTEEN

MIRACLES OF SALVATION

"For the wages of sin is death; but the gift of God is eternal life through Jesus Christ our Lord."
Romans 3:23,

PLAN OF SALVATION

If you have read this book and you don't know Jesus Christ as your personal Lord and savior, then read the Plan of Salvation and if you once knew the Lord Jesus Christ as your Lord and Savior and backslid then pray the prayer of Faith for your Miracle of restoration. One of the greatest Miracles is the Miracle of Salvation. The bibles says the whole of heaven rejoice when one soul come to repentance. If ever you're going to receive that miracle which you are believing God for, you first have to accept the miracle worker and his name is JESUS. The bible also says that believe and you shall received.

First: The Bible declares: "I am come that they might have life and that they might have it more abundantly"

(John 10:10). Giving you abundant life required the supreme sacrifice: "For God so loved the world that he gave his only begotten Son, that whosoever believeth in him should not perish, but have everlasting life" (John 3:16). God desires fellowship and companionship with you. What a wonderful gift the Father has given; yet if God gave His own Son to provide an abundant and everlasting life, why don't more people have what He has designed for us to receive? It is a question answered by this sobering realization.

Second: There is a gap between God and mankind. He has provided a way for us to receive an abundant and eternal life, but people throughout the ages have made selfish choices to disobey God Almighty. These choices continue to cause separation form the Father. God's Word shows us that the result of sin is death. He says in His Word: "There is a way which seemeth right unto a man, but the end thereof is the ways of death" (Proverbs 14:12). And God also said, "But your iniquities have separated between you and your God, and sins have hid his face from you, that he will not hear" (Isaiah 59:2). Paul the apostle states in Romans 3:23, "For the wages of sin is death; but the gift of God is eternal life through Jesus Christ our Lord." Every human was created with the ability and need to know God and fellowship with Him. Augustine, a minister who lived during the fourth and fifth centuries, called this longing in each of us "That God-shaped vacuum." Every day we hear of people who are rich, famous, achievers, star athletes—people who seem to have the best that life can offer—yet they try to fill that empty void in their lives with things. They even try good works, morality, and religion. Yet they remain empty, for only God, through His Son, can fill that emptiness.

Third: Jesus Christ, His Son, is the only way to God. Only He can reconcile us to God the Father. Mankind may seek other solutions and worship other gods, but Jesus Christ, alone, died on the Cross for our sins and rose in triumph over the grave and eternal death. He paid the penalty for our sin and bridged the gap between God and mankind. The Bible explains: "But God commendeth his love toward us, in that, while we were yet sinners, Christ died for us" (Romans 5:8). We are also told, "For Christ also hath once suffered for sins, the just for the unjust, that he might bring us to God" (1 Peter 3:18). There is only one way provided: "For there is one God, and one mediator between God and men, the man Christ Jesus" (1 Timothy 2:5). For in John 14:6 we read, "Jesus saith unto him, I am the way, the truth, and the life: no man cometh unto the Father, but by me." God Almighty has provided the only way. Jesus Christ paid the penalty for our sin and rebellion against God by dying on the cross, shedding His blood, and rising from the dead to justify and reconcile you back to God the Father.

Fourth: You can be brought back to God, and your relationship with Him can be restored by trusting in Christ alone to save your life from destruction. What an incredible exchange: Your worst for God's best! This step happens by asking Jesus Christ to take away your sin and to come into your heart to be your Lord and Savior. God's Word is very clear: "Behold, I stand at the door, and knock: if any man hear my voice, and open the door, I will come in to him, and will sup with him, and he with me" (Revelation 3:20). And the Bible tells us, "That if thou shalt confess with thy mouth the Lord Jesus, and shalt believe in thine heart that God hath raised him form the dead, thou shalt be saved" (Romans 10:9). Are you willing to let go of your burdens and sins? Are you willing to turn away and repent form your sins? Are you willing to receive Jesus Christ as your Lord and Savior now?

CHAPTER FOURTEEN

PRAYER OF FAITH FOR SALVATION AND RESTORATION

O Father God in Heaven, I come to you because I need your forgiveness. I have done wrong. I confess to you all my sins. I deserve to die for them. I cannot save myself. But I thank you for dying on the cross to take away the guilt and evil in my life. Jesus, save me! Cleanse me! Forgive me! I believe in my heart that God raised you from the dead. From now on I receive you and confess you openly as my Lord, Master and Savior. I receive the gift of righteousness from you by faith. Change me Jesus more and more each day to be like you. Be Lord of my spirit, soul and body. Break the power of sin from my life.

As you forgive me, I now forgive all that have hurt me. I turn away from all evil. I renounce Satan and any areas of influence he has in me for any reason (name the areas you know about). In the name of Jesus Christ I command all evil power to leave me now. I purpose now to never accept your evil powers back in my life.

I thank you Father that I am now a child of God through faith in Jesus Christ. I am born again. I am a new person. My sins are forgiven. I am part of the Kingdom of God. Jesus Christ lives in me and through me. Thank you Father for the gift of eternal life!

Dear Holy Spirit, I trust you to lead me in the Word of God and prayer every day. Help me to obey the voice of God and fully accomplish God's purposes for my life. Amen.

SCRIPTURE READING

Read all these wonderful scriptures that will help you to grow in Christ.

Luke 15:21; 1 John 1:8-9; Romans 6:23; Galatians 3:10-11; Romans 10:13; 1 John 1:9; 1 Peter 2:24; 3:18; Romans 10:9,10; Romans 5:17; 2 Corinthians 3:18; 1 Thessalonians 5:23; Romans 6:6; Hebrews 7:25; Matthew 6:14,15; Matthew 6:13; James 4:7; Mark 16:17; Galatians 3:26; John 3:3; 2 Corinthians 5:17; 1 John 2:12; Romans 14:17; Galatians 2:20; John 3:16)

By praying this prayer, confessing your sins, and receiving Jesus Christ into your heart, God has given you the right to become His forgiven child. The Bible gives you this assurance: "But as many as received him, to them he gave the power to become the sons of God, even to them who believe on his name." (John1:12).

If you have just received Jesus Christ into your life, we would like to rejoice with you. As such, please send us an email to my ministry at testimony@robinhealingministry.com.

GLORY BE TO GOD THE FATHER, HIS SON JESUS AND THE HOLY SPIRIT.

AMEN.

NOTES

NOTES

NOTES

NOTES

Printed in the United States
201869BV00002B/229-1023/A